THE
RHYTHM OF THE
REDMAN

*In Song, Dance
and Decoration*

BY

JULIA M. BUTTREE

Y

*Introduction,
Art Section and Illustrations*
by

ERNEST THOMPSON SETON

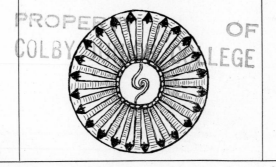

New York
A. S. BARNES AND COMPANY
INCORPORATED
1930

11931

PRINTED IN THE UNITED STATES OF AMERICA

Introduction

INDIAN DANCING

By ERNEST THOMPSON SETON

When our women cut off their skirts and threw away their corsets, they entered a new and saner epoch of life and joy. They raised not only themselves, but their offspring and the whole nation, to a higher level of physical vigor and morality.

It is very hard for the present generation to realize the deplorable—yes, the shocking—condition of women in the mid-Victorian period. Woman was then assumed to be an angel; she had no legs, functions, or emotions,—she was supposed to be solid from the waist down. The crinoline came at the climax of these follies. For a woman to show a hint of an ankle was to be socially and eternally damned.

The theory was, further, that every woman had a wasp waist and a small, pointed foot. To keep the feminine world in line with these ideals, each woman was panoplied in a steel corset that squeezed the body to the desired shape at the expense of her vital organs. Her foot was forced into an excruciatingly hard shoe of metal and leather that crushed it out of all natural form into a sharp pointed mangled remains, atrophied, nearly useless as a foot, loathsome with corns and agonized with bunions.

And what was the sum total of result? Every woman was more or less of an invalid,—not only was, but persistently claimed and announced it. The robust health of the working woman was despised as vulgar; and all women were divided into delicate and indelicate. Swooning was taught in the young ladies' seminaries as a necessary and important activity. Languishing Lydia was the ideal; and no woman of good social standing could walk a mile or swim a stroke. In order to further guarantee her helplessness, every woman of any position dragged a dress train, even in the streets, amid the horse-filth of the roadway.

The race might well have been nipped out by these suicidal obsessions. But it was saved, we believe, by the swamping influence of the athletic other sex, and the reinvigorating blood of the peasant class inevitably working upward, as the fashionable families killed themselves off.

These demoralizing ideals of life and clothing were all-powerful in the Victorian epoch. The first little gap in their entrenched position was made by the game of tennis.

But the real defeat was inflicted by the bicycle. About 1890, all the world went wheeling-mad. Girls wanted to go a-wheeling with their brothers,—but could not in long trailing garments. Various devices were produced to meet the difficulty, but nothing satisfactory till, in France, the *bicyclettes*, or knickers for girls, were boldly proclaimed and worn. In spite of a storm of indignation from intrenched prudery, they were commercially launched here; backed by commonsense and by hygiene, they passed all the stages of shock, wrath, scorn and ridicule— and were at last quietly accepted.

The abandonment of corsets, tight shoes, and impossible collars, came in quick succession. Woman was admitted to have legs, functions, and emotions, just as much as her brother. The clothing reform was well on the way; and, for the first time in modern history, woman was blessed with the robust health that had hitherto been considered the exclusive birthright of her brothers.

Now, we were confronted with a new situation, a new thought. It is a law of nature that sentient, highly organized beings, when blessed with abundant physical vigor, joy, and opportunity, must express their exhilaration in a dance, preferably to music; but always an energetic, rhythmic dance.

The new-found vigor of our females and the thereby increased vigor of our males, with growing insistence demanded general and vigorous dancing. We had, of course, such purely artificial things as the minuet, quadrille, etc., and the waltz still under ban. But none of these were athletic, rhythmic exercise, possible for all, easily, and at almost any time.

Two responses appeared to meet the demand—the fox-trot and its kind from South America, and the Greek dancing of the Duncan School. The unloveliness of the first group, with its over-emphasis on sex, has gradually abolished it. The Greek dances, although beautiful, poetic, and admirable, were the rare activity of a trained few; furthermore, although graceful posing, they never were vigorous, rhythmic exercise. They still are, perforce, the activity of the more or less professional.

Later came the Charleston and Black Bottom, invented by a race that, at least, had rhythm, and sought for exercise with musical accompaniment. But, for obvious reasons, these too have passed away.

Folk dancing of the European nations was revived; but has not been a complete success, because the dances are either too complex, too childish, or call for too much space and preparation. Furthermore there is little or no appeal to the imagination.

Not one of these types of dancing fills the bill.

Where are we to find the much needed leader in acceptable dancing? In my opinion, that leader is the North American Indian. Nationally speaking, he is the best dancer in the world today. That does not mean that he is better than our professional stage dancers—undoubtedly, *they* are the best. But these are not national; they are specially gifted groups, selected and trained.

I have seen Russian, French, Spanish, Italian, Hungarian, Scottish, Irish, and English dances, both in their homes and in their stage presentation. And still I affirm, without fear of challenge, that better than any of these as a dancer is the North American Indian. His dancing is clean, beautiful, dramatic, interpretive, rhythmic exercise; it is possible for all, and is meritorious according to the gift of the dancer. But always it is in some degree, good,—it is wonderful, beautiful exercise.

More than any other, it carries us out of doors; and finds its best presentation in the camp life that is happily becoming a dominating mode in our present thought.

Calling for, and exhibiting more than any other dancing the perfection of physique, it is helping us to regain the noblest ideals of outdoor life that did so much for ancient Greece.

Appealing to the imagination as well as to the muscles, it is, in the highest sense, educational. Untainted with sex, hallowed always by a thought of prayer, and vivid with rejoicing, it is, above all, the exercise of a clean people, voicing their gladness as a conscious, harmonious part of the joyous sunlit world.

Can one feel so about any of our modern dances? Imagine a waltz or a polka in camp about the sacred fire. When King David "danced with all his might" about the Ark of the Lord, he certainly did not dance a minuet or a schottische, but a joyous, ecstatic, spiritual rhythm, that was in all its elements, an Indian dance.

It was with a view to perpetuating these human rhythms for our own people, that the many expeditions, especially that of 1927, were made into the Indian world, the condensed results of which are offered in the present volume.

Table of Contents

List of Illustrations

xi

GRADED LIST OF DANCES

I

II

III

Theme

I have "seen the Red Man dancing
To sustain the World Throb penned
Alive between his ribs,
Not like a ballerina's, in her toes,
But next to where his life is,
Heart, breath, and bowels of him; moved
With the desire to make the world work well with God."
—MARY AUSTIN, *The American Rhythm*, p. 140.

Why Dance?

Dancing is a universal instinct,—a zoölogic, a biologic impulse, found in animals as well as in man. At first thought, one would say the higher animals; but most of us have watched the whirligig water-bugs on a hot summer afternoon, pirouetting wildly about, winding in and out among each other on the surface, in every direction and with the greatest speed, yet never colliding. The mayflies, creatures of a day, enjoy their brief, merry love-dance in the air, and at its climax, die.

Among the birds, there are the sage grouse, the pinnated grouse, the cock o' the rock, the woodcock, the teals with their stately minuet, and the ruffed grouse which not only parades, but drums his own accompaniment.

A still more interesting incident is furnished by Ernest Thompson Seton in *The Dance of the Pintailed Grouse*. I quote from his unpublished autobiography:

"In the summer of 1883, at Carberry, Manitoba, I had some fifteen baby Prairie Chickens hatched under a hen. When they were two weeks old, we were visited by a cold driving storm of sleet. The chicks were in danger of perishing.

"I brought the whole brood into the kitchen. Keeping the hen in a cage close by, I put the chilled and cowering little things under the stove, on the tin which protected the floor. Here, after half an hour, they were fully warmed. They recovered quickly, fluffed out their feathers, preened their wings, and began to look very perky.

"Then the clouds broke. For the first time that day, the sun shone brightly. It came through the window, down onto the stove, and partly under, on the assembled brood.

"It seemed to stir them with some new thought and feeling of joy. One of the tiny things, no bigger than a sparrow, lowered his head nearly to the tin, with beak out level, raised high the little pimple where in time his tail should be, spread out at each side his tiny wings; then ran across the tin, crowing a little bubbling crow, beating his wings, and stamping with his two pink feet so rapidly that it sounded like a small kettledrum.

"The result was electrical. At once, the rest of them leaped up and at it. Every one took the same position—head low, wings out, beating, tail-stump raised and violently vibrated, the feet pounding hard, as the little dancers crowed and careered in, about, over, and amid the others—crowing, leaping, bounding, stamping, exactly as is done by the old birds on the dance hill at love-time.

I

"For a minute or more it lasted; then they seemed tired, and all sat down for a rest.

"In half an hour, they were at it again; and did it several times that day, more especially when the sun was on them, and they were warm and fed.

"Then I found that I could start them when the conditions were right, by rattling on the tin a tattoo with two fingers. They responded almost invariably; during the three days that I had them in the house, I started them dancing many times for myself or the neighborhood to see. A number of my friends made a buggy drive across country those days to come and see the tiny downlings 'do their war dance,' whenever I chose to start them by beating the drum.

"It is noteworthy that these chickens danced exactly as their parents do, without ever having seen those parents; therefore, the performance was wholly instinctive. All—and undoubtedly both sexes were repre-sented—danced with equal spirit. It was not at the breeding season, and could not, in any sense, be said to have any sex urge. It was evi-dently and unquestionably nothing more nor less than a true dance—a vigorous, rhythmic, athletic expression of health and joy."

Dance in the Animal World

So far, it is chiefly the birds that are credited with song and dance. But added observations continually extend the field. Many, if not all the higher animals have some related exercise.

You remember Kipling's elephant, which escaped from camp at night, and trotted on and on till he came to the appointed place of meeting. Here he and his kind danced the greater part of the night—a true social gathering. The story of Mowgli may be fiction; but there is good evidence that this incident is founded on fact.

The wapiti have been seen by several hunters to engage in a circle dance, which has no obvious explanation other than the pleasure of the motion. They have been reported "in a band of from twelve to twenty . . . trotting quite rapidly, with occasional awkward plunges, in a circle perhaps thirty feet in diameter. They were all going in the same direction as the hands of a watch." (H. W. Skinner, quoted by Ernest Thompson Seton in his *Lives*, III, p. 42.)

The most remarkable of all, perhaps, is the *Kanjo* of the chimpanzees, described by R. L. Garner. The chimpanzees select a spot in the jungle about two feet across, where the surface of the ground is peat. They secure some clay along the banks of a nearby stream, carry it by hand, spread it over the place, and let it dry. When all is hard, the chimpanzees gather in great numbers. One or two violently beat this hard clay which gives out a loud sound. The others "jump up and down in a wild and grotesque manner. Some of them make long rolling sounds, as if trying to sing. When one tires of beating the drum, another relieves him, and the festivities continue in this fashion for hours." (*Gorillas and Chimpanzees*, pp. 59-60.)

Dancing Among Savages

Among men, savages are nearly all great dancers, imitating every animal they know, and dancing out their own legends. The South Sea Islanders, the Zulus, the negroes of Central Africa, and the native Australians, are all practicing it now exactly as it was in the earlier stages of every civilized race. In its natural, primitive form, dancing is vigorous muscular action to vent emotion. Originally, it was the natural expression of the basic impulses of a simple form of life. Triumph, defeat, war, love, hate, desire, propitiation of the gods—all were danced by the hero or the tribe to the rhythm of beaten drums.

3

The history of dancing goes back farther than we can accurately trace it. But we do know that in very ancient times, in China, the spring was ushered in with dance and ritual; all boys after the age of thirteen were taught dancing as an important part of their education.

In Japan, in ancient Rome, in Egypt, and in Greece, dancing was a form of worship. The old philosophers ranked it with poetry and drama. The Spartans made it a compulsory part of the education of all children from the age of five.

At a very early period, the Hebrews gave dancing a high place in their ceremony of worship. Moses bade the children of Israel to dance after the crossing of the Red Sea. Miriam danced to a song of triumph, and David danced in a procession before the Ark of the Covenant.

Among the early Christians, it was universally introduced into religious services. The bishops of those days led the sacred dance around the altar.

It has been shown that the choral processions, with all the added charm of costume and song, have had far more to do with Christianizing primitive tribes, than has preaching.

During the Dark Ages of history, dancing was taken under the protection of the Church, through which it survived during the greater part of a thousand years. The vehicle which carried it through this period was the Spectacle and Miracle or Mystery plays.

After this, dancing gradually withdrew from the Church, until, under Louis XIV, it reached a high development as a secular and social amusement.

Value of Dancing

The power of the dance is universal, both in time and place. It is confined to no one country of the world, to no period of ancient or modern history, and to no plane of human culture.

Its value has always been felt, though often used without conscious appreciation of its worth. It is a powerful agency to conjure up emotion of one kind or another. Ferocious war dances were practiced by savage tribes, in order to beget the war frenzy which should carry them irresistibly on to victory. The dancing and spinning dervishes of the East hypnotize themselves with a delirium of physical excitement as a stepping stone to excesses of religious zeal and self-sacrifice.

I have frequently used dancing with classes of obstreperous children, to induce mental states more in harmony with my purposes of teaching.

There was a time when we had to fight for the principle that dancing was a desirable activity—essential, inevitable. We had to argue for the right to manifest, or even to possess, the joy of living. But that day is gone. Psychologists and educators in all fields appreciate the power and necessity of dancing, wisely selected. It is surely safe to say that the

4

only persons who now disapprove of dancing, rightly inspired, are those who have never studied it, nor its reaction upon the physical, mental, spiritual and social well-being of the individual and group.

The problem now is what to select as the best kind of dancing for our developmental purpose. To the outdoor educator, after nothing less than world-wide search, there can be no question that the ideal we seek is found in but one type of dancing—the dancing of the American Indian.

In the Redman's dance, or its adaptation, we find the physical exercise, the dramatic and imaginative possibilities, the impelling rhythm, and the picturesqueness, all combined, which the youth of our country are groping for in their blind way, among other schools of the art.

Indian Dancing

The importance of the dance in the life of the Indian is shown in the fact that his most elaborate ceremonies are commonly known as dances.

The Indians teach a child to dance as soon as it can be held erect, training it to lift its little feet with the motion of a dancer, and instilling a sense of rhythm from the very beginning. In the CORN DANCE which we witnessed at Santo Domingo, one of the chorus carried a baby, perhaps three months old, upright against him all day, as he kept vigorous time to the rhythm of the music.

In the early stages of thought, the dance was inseparable from the song or chant. Now, the songs are usually sung by the men who play the accompanying instruments. If the dancers move in a circle, the instruments are placed in the center of the circle; otherwise they are in a row at one side.

The dances are many; but each has its name, its steps and movements, and its special songs; each has its history, and usually its symbolism, though much of this latter has been lost in civilization and self-consciousness.

There are dances for men and women together; and other dances in which men and women dance by themselves; still others in which individuals dance alone.

There are comic dances, and dances in costumes that disguise the persons taking part. Many employ masks symbolic in both form and color. In some tribes feathers are the principal decoration; in some, the men dance nearly nude.

But, however diverse the dancing regalia may be, or how marked its absence, no matter what the purpose of the dance, or the steps used, the Indian dance always presents two characteristics—dramatic action and rhythmic precision.

Dances of great activity are done exclusively by the men. Usually the dance is performed in a small space, or even on one spot. The changes of attitude, however, are sometimes rapid and violent. When the Indian dances, he dances with freedom, and every movement is vivid and natural. This is, perhaps, the most significant difference between the dances of the Red and White man. Our dance action has become conventional to the last degree—in all except the modern ballroom dancing, where a little more convention might be desired.

An Indian has said: "The White man dances with his legs; the Indian with his individual muscles." His dance, is, certainly, rather a body vibration than a limb motion.

The Makah Indians of Washington have a great number of what we would call interpretive dances; and it was not unusual in this tribe for a woman to dance alone. But, in most tribes, the women were not solo dancers, and did not employ the violent steps and forceful attitudes of the men's dances.

Hartley B. Alexander says: "The steps [of the women] are mincing, feet hardly lifted from the ground, the elbows close to the body and the hands barely shaken, the face impassive; yet noted closely, it will be seen that the whole flesh is quivering with the rhythm of the drum. Such dancing can be imitated only in a sketchlike fashion; the art itself is not the white man's." (*Manitou Masks*, p. 15.)

Alice Corbin Henderson says: the dances "are the heart and core of Pueblo life; they represent the incarnation of the Pueblo soul. When the Pueblo Indian fights for his dances, he is fighting for his soul. . . . If we help the Pueblo artist to find his soul, we may find our own."

And again: "The spirit of these dances is so pure, so genuine; they spring so inevitably from a primal source, that a comparison with our more artificial art is almost impossible." (*Dance Rituals of the Pueblo Indians*.)

When a certain Wild West showman was putting on Indian dancers, doing weird barbaric hopping, yelling, and brandishing of spears, he was asked by one who knew how false such a demonstration was: "Why do you do that? You know that that is not the real Indian dancing." He replied: "Sure, I know. But that's what the public thinks is Indian dancing, so I must give it to them."

It is from such sensational sources that most of us obtained our first ideas of the art. How absurdly false such presentations are, and what a real loss they inflict, I slowly realized. It was not until the summer of 1927 that I had the full opportunity of seeing for myself what a new world of joyful art was open to those who study Indian dancing. Before that memorable trip was over, we had seen among the Indians not only the steps of nearly all other nations, but many that were peculiar to the Redman; as well as these steps combined into numberless characteristic and beautiful dances. We saw, in all, sixty-eight dances and had twenty more described to us by authorities. There are literally hundreds of different dances among the Redmen. It is safe to say of these that they embody all the advantages of our social and exhibition dances, and eliminate the grosser faults.

In the dances which follow, those that I have *actually recorded*, are as true to their presentation as is in my power to make them. The *adaptations* are combinations of authentic steps, woven into routines which may appeal to our White modes of thought. In such, I have generally made the story more apparent than it was in the Indian dance which suggested the adaptation. To the Indian, the symbolism of his gestures

7

is clear. But these have been handed down through generations, and have become so stereotyped that they are difficult, and in many cases, impossible, of translation.

In these adaptations, I have endeavored to be faithful to good Indian attitudes of mind and pose; but have made little attempt to be ethnologically correct. I have freely borrowed and combined material, aiming to present a *racial* rather than a *tribal* dance; desiring also, from a study of the characteristics, to create a dance form which will be pregnant with suggestion to our individual dancers, a dance impression of authentic interpretation rather than slavish photographic reproduction.

I wish to offer sincere thanks to the many publications listed in my bibliography; they have been of inestimable value in the formulation of the book; also to Dr. G. Clyde Fisher of the American Museum of Natural History, and to Carol Stryker of the Staten Island Museum, and to the Mack Photo Service of Santa Fe, for the use of their photographs of Indian dances.

But, at this point, I make most grateful acknowledgment to the two women who, in my mind, have done more to bring the Redman into his own than all the rest of his advocates put together—and this, by recognizing the fact that the best defense for the Redman's art was to faithfully reproduce it in language that even Whites can understand. Frances Densmore and Natalie Curtis, in their books of Indian songs, have helped us to an appreciation of the art that is illuminating. I have literally lived with these books for the past year; and have been inspired again and again to a new dance thought by their presentation of a song or a legend. I urgently recommend them to all interested in Indian lore, as storehouses of otherwise unavailable treasures.

PART ONE
INDIAN DANCES

Fundamental Steps

1. *Step Drag-Close* (Fig. 1)

Counts

1. Long step to right.
2. Bring left up to right, dragging it along ground
    Repeat to cover the required distance.

Fig. 1.

2. *Step Lift-Close*

1. Long step to right
2. Bring left up to right, lifting it clear of ground
    Repeat to cover the required distance.

3. *Shuffle*

1. On ball of right foot, drag to right a very short distance
&. On ball of left foot, drag to right a very short distance
2. As 1
&. As & above
    This is done very rapidly, as fast as you can count and may be
    done to right, to left, forward, or backward.

4. *Front Trot*

1.   Jump on to right foot, lifting left knee high in front
2.   Jump on to left foot, bringing right knee high in front

Repeat for required time, but with frequent holds for one count, with one knee held high through two counts.

5. *Back Trot* (Fig. 2)

1.   Jump on to right foot, bending left knee, and holding left foot high in back

FIG. 2.

2.   Jump on to left foot, bending right knee, and holding right foot high in back

Repeat for required time, but with frequent holds for one count, with one foot held high through two counts.

6. *Toe-Flat* (Fig. 3)

1.   Step forward on left toe
&.   Drop left heel in place
2.   Step forward on right toe
&.   Drop right heel in place

Repeat as often as necessary. This is a good rest step, to be injected between two more strenuous steps.

Counts

1.   Hop on left, at same time turning right leg over and touching right toe to floor at right oblique back, heel in air

&.   Hop on left foot, at same time turning right leg over and touching right heel to floor at right oblique back, toe in air

2.   Hop on right foot, at same time turning left leg over and touching left toe to floor at left oblique back, heel in air

&.   Hop on right foot, at same time turning left leg over and touching left heel to floor at left oblique back, toe in air

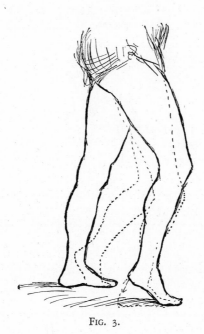

Fig. 3.

8. Heel-Toe

1.   Right heel forward, bending left knee a little

&.   Point right toe, straightening left knee

2.   Left heel forward, bending right knee a little

&.   Point left toe, straightening right knee

This may be used as a rest step. It may progress forward or backward.

9. *Heel-Flat*

1.   Right heel forward, bending left knee a little
&.   Draw right foot backward, dropping the toe
2.   Left heel forward, bending right knee a little
&.   Draw left foot backward, dropping the toe
     This may be done in place, or progress forward or backward, according to the distance covered in the draw-back.

10. *Cross Toe-Flat*

1.   Cross left over right, stepping on left toe
&.   Drop left heel, at same time swinging right foot out to right
2.   Cross right over left, stepping on right toe
&.   Drop right heel, at same time swinging left foot out to left
     This is best done in place, without any progression, though distance can be covered by making one cross-step longer than the other.

11. *Toe-Flat Cross*

1.   Step right toe to right
&.   Drop right heel
2.   Cross left toe over to right of right
&.   Drop left heel
     This makes a progression to the right. If movement to left is desired, start on left toe to left.

12. *Flat-Heel* (Fig. 4)

1.   Step forward with flat right, bending both knees a little
&.   Lift and drop the right heel, straightening both knees with a snap
2.   Step forward with flat left, bending both knees a little
&.   Lift and drop the left heel, straightening both knees with a snap
     This is a little difficult to acquire; but when the swing is once mastered, is a very useful step.

13. *Toe-Tap-Tap-Heel*

1.   Step right toe forward
&.   Left heel tap
2.   Left heel tap
&.   Drop right heel in place
1.   Step left toe forward
&.   Right heel tap
2.   Right heel tap
&.   Drop left heel in place

14. *Step-Tap-Tap-Tap*

Counts

1.	Step left forward
&.	Point back with right
2.	Point back with right
&.	Step back with right
3.	Step left forward
&.	Point forward with right
4.	Point forward with right
&.	Step forward with right

15. *Cross-Hop*

1.	Cross right over left
&.	Hop on right

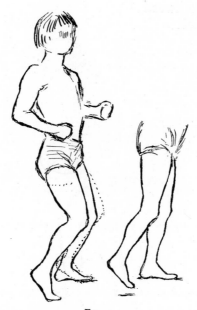

FIG. 4.

2.	Cross left over right
&.	Hop on left

This may be done in place, or with progression in any direction. A good step, and easily acquired.

16. Toe-Flat Rock

Counts

1. Point forward with right
&. Drop right flat
2. Point backward with left
&. Drop left flat

This constitutes a rocking, and is a good step with which to remain in same spot.

17. Toe-Flat Zigzag

1. Point forward with right
&. Drop right heel
2. Point left backward
&. Drop left heel
3. Point right forward
&. Drop right heel
4. Point left forward
&. Drop left heel
5. Point right backward
&. Drop right heel

Fig. 5.

6. Point left forward
&. Drop left heel
7. Point right forward
&. Drop right heel
8. Point left backward
&. Drop left heel

16

18. *Three-point Drop* (Fig. 5)

1. Point forward right
2. Repeat
3. Repeat
4. Drop right flat

Repeat, starting with other foot. This is a preparation for the next step.

19. *Five-point Pivot*

1. Step forward with flat right
2. Tap with left to back
3. Tap with left to left oblique back
4. Tap with left to left
5. Tap with left to left oblique front
6. Tap with left to front

Drop left heel, and repeat taps with right foot. As the taps progress, pivot on the still foot toward the direction of the still foot. That is, when the left foot is tapping, the pivot is toward the right, making a half-circle until the left heel drops, when the pivot starts to the left, the right foot tapping.

20. *Forward, Forward, Back, Back*

1. Step forward left
&. Step forward right
2. Step backward left
&. Step backward right

21. *Sneak Step*

1. Step to right with right toe, knees a little bent
&. Step to right with left toe, crossing in front of right (Fig. 6)
2. Step to right with right toe, uncrossing
&. Step to right with left toe, crossing in back of right (Fig. 7)

This makes for progression to the right. If movement to left is desired, start with left toe to left.

22. *Cross Slide*

1. Cross left in front of right
&. Slide back on left, lifting right from ground
2. Cross right in front of left
&. Slide back on right, lifting left from ground

23. *Rock and Hop* (Fig. 8 and 9)

Counts

1. Balance forward on right toe
&. Balance back on left foot
2. Balance forward on right toe
&. Hop on right foot, swinging left forward

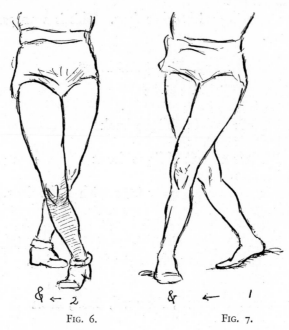

FIG. 6.   FIG. 7.

3. Balance forward on left toe
&. Balance back on right foot
4. Balance forward on left toe
&. Hop on left foot, swinging right forward

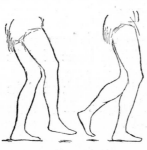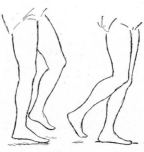

FIG. 8.   FIG. 9.

5. Balance forward on right toe
&. Balance back on left foot
6. Balance forward on right toe
&. Balance back on left foot

7.   Balance forward on right toe
&.   Balance back on left foot
8.   Balance forward on right toe
&.   Hop on right foot, swinging left forward
    Keep the body loose throughout.

24. *The Sioux Limp*

1.   Step left to left
&.   Draw right to left, bending the knees a little with a snap, at the same time lifting the left heel
2.   Step left to left
&.   Draw right to left, bending the knees a little with a snap, at the same time lifting the left heel
    This may be done also to right, or forward, or backward. It is very tiresome to the foot which does the drawing if properly done.

25. *Step Hop Hop*

1.   Step right to right
2.   Hop on right
3.   Hop on right

FIG. 10.

1.   Step left to left
2.   Hop on left
3.   Hop on left

26. *Sioux Hop-step* (Fig. 10)

Counts

1. Step forward with right
&. Hop on right, keeping left toe turned up, and raising left foot up in front of ankle (not backward as in our hopping). Progress forward, backward, or around self

27. *Hop-point Step*

1. Hop on left and point with right, feet landing close together, right foot about three inches in advance of left
2. Step on right
1. Hop on right and point with left, as above
2. Step on left

28. *High Hop-point* (Fig. 11)

&. Hop on left, at same time raising right knee high in front
1. Tap with right toe, feet close together

Fig. 11.

&. Hop on left, at same time raising right knee high in front
2. Tap with right toe, feet close together

Progression may be in any direction, but the feet do not alternate. The tapping is always on the right foot.

29. *Front Ankle Hold*

1.   Hop on right foot, crossing left foot in front of right ankle
&.   Repeat
2.   Repeat
&.   Repeat

Repeat, starting with left hop.

30. *Back Ankle Hold*

1.   Hop on right foot, crossing left foot in back of right ankle
&.   Repeat
2.   Repeat
&.   Repeat

Repeat, starting with left hop.

31. *Front Calf Hold*

1.   Hop on right foot, crossing left foot in front of right calf
&.   Repeat
2.   Repeat
&.   Repeat

Repeat, starting with left hop.

32. *Back Calf Hold*

1.   Hop on right foot, crossing left foot in back of right calf
&.   Repeat
2.   Repeat
&.   Repeat

Repeat, starting with left hop.

33. *Front Knee Hold*

1.   Hop on right foot, crossing left foot in front of right knee
&.   Repeat
2.   Repeat
&.   Repeat

Repeat, starting with left hop.

34. *Back Knee Hold*

1.   Hop on right foot, crossing left foot in back of right knee
&.   Repeat
2.   Repeat
&.   Repeat

Repeat, starting with left hop.

Two feet close together, and worked simultaneously, knees well bent, jump to right, right, right; or left, left, left; or forward, forward, forward.

36. *Cross-Step-Cross-Hop*

1. Cross right over left
&. Step left to left
2. Cross right over left
&. Hop on right

Repeat, starting with left crossed over right.

37. *Pivot*

Low bent, shading eyes with hand, pivot, one foot still, other pushing with short sharp steps.

FIG. 12.

38. *Scare Step* (Fig. 12)

1. Cross right in front of left, bending both knees a little
&. Step left a little to left, but still keeping feet crossed
2. Step right farther to left
&. Step left a little to left, still crossed
3. Step right farther to left
&. Step left a little to left, still crossed

4.   Step right farther to left
&.   Hop on right

Repeat, starting on other foot.

When right is crossed in front, the head is turned to the right, and both hands, palms out, are to the right, as if warding off something from that direction. This pose is held throughout the four counts, then changes with the feet.

39. *Women's Step* (Fig. 13)

Start with feet close together; both toes raised, and turned slightly to the right.

1.   Drop the toes, and bend the knees at the same time
&.   Swing on the balls of the feet, so the heels turn to the right, straighten the knees, and drop back on the heels
2.   Swing on the heels so the toes turn to the right, drop the toes and bend the knees

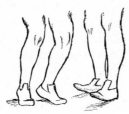

FIG. 13.

&.   Swing on the balls, so the heels turn to the right, straighten the knees, and drop back on the heels

Skim along the ground with this step, alternately swaying the shoulders in unison with the feet.

Mountain Chant of the Navaho

This is a nine days' ceremony of healing, dramatizing the myth of the Navaho tribal history. It has been described at great length by Dr. Washington Mathews, in the *Fifth Ethnological Report* (pub. 1887), pp. 385-467.

Natalie Curtis records one song from the MOUNTAIN CHANT in her *Indians' Book*, p. 408. This I have used in the following routine, based exactly on the DOLL DANCE which I saw at Gallup in the August of 1927.

Miss Curtis gives the following legend as the basis of the ceremony:

"The Holy Youth, Tsilchke Digini, loved a mortal maid; and, to make her divine like himself, so that he might take her to wife, he sang holy songs over her. Thenceforth she was called Estsan Digini, the Holy Woman. Together the two gave these songs to the Navahos, to be used by them as a cure for sickness."

The song is sung in two stanzas, identical, except that the first stanza pertains to the male divinity, and the second to the female. In the second stanza, substitute "she" for "he."

DSICHOYIDJE HATAL	SONG FROM THE MOUNTAIN CHANT
Baiyajiltriyish,	Thereof he telleth,
Tsilchke digini, Baiyajiltriyish.	Now of the Holy Youth, Thereof he telleth.
Ke-pa-nashjini, Baiyajiltriyish.	Moccasins decked with black, Thereof he telleth.
Kla-pa-naskan-a, Baiyajiltriyish.	And richly broidered dress, Thereof he telleth.
Ka' ka pa-stran-a, Baiyajiltriyish.	Arm-bands of eagle feathers, Thereof he telleth.
Niltsan stsoz-i, Baiyajiltriyish.	And now the rain-plumes, Thereof he telleth.
Niltsan-bekan-a, Baiyajiltriyish.	Now of the Male-Rain, Thereof he telleth.

DSICHOYIDJE HATAL	SONG FROM THE MOUNTAIN CHANT
Ka' bi datro-e, Baiyajiltriyish.	Now of the rain-drops fallen Thereof he telleth.
Sa-a naraï, Baiyajiltriyish.	Now of the Unending Life, Thereof he telleth.
Bike hozhoni, Baiyajiltriyish.	Now of Unchanging Joy, Thereof he telleth.
Baiyajiltriyish.	Thereof he telleth.

The Male-Rain is the heavy storm-rain, with lightning and thunder; the Female-Rain is the gentle shower. Both kinds of rain are prized in sickness for their cooling power.

The Doll Dance

This is one of the dances of the MOUNTAIN CHANT.

There is a small fire in the center of the dance space. Enter in ordinary Navaho costume (see Fig. 14 for description), two men carrying rattles, one carrying a flat basketry tray, two with a feather each in the right hand, and two elaborately dressed, impersonating dolls with wonderful headdresses. These last two are the Holy Youth and the Holy

FIG. 14.

Woman. They carry in each hand a framework about 15 inches wide, topping a stick, as in Fig. 15. The whole is 12-14 inches high, and is hung with many ribbons.

The step used for the entrance, indeed for the whole dance of the main group, is: Step sidewise left (1-2); close right up to left (3). The side step is done with a slight sidewise dip.

With the same step, the group encircles the fire	19 meas.
With the same step in forward progression, they move in to the fire	4 meas.
They back outward from the fire	4 meas.
Repeat the last two until 24 measures are used in all	16 meas.

26

As they approach the fire, the hands are raised toward the sky; as they back out, they are lowered toward the ground.

The group stand still in place, except the bearer of the basket, who places it to one side; then all but the two dolls approach it, using the same step as above. The two feathers are set up in the basket, four of the chorus sit about it, all facing the center; the rest stand to one side and sing   8 meas.

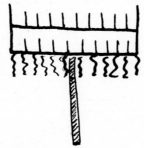

Hand Frame Doll Dance

FIG. 15.

The two dolls now shuffle in from opposite sides, approaching until they face each other, with the basket between them on the ground.

They shuffle toward the fire   4 meas.

Shuffle out from the fire   4 meas.

Shuffle in toward the fire   4 meas.

They now dance opposite each other, with much high knee stepping, prancing occasionally to one side or the other. The feathers, evidently manipulated with horsehairs by the four sitters, imitate the action of the dancers, until the music ends in a wail   72 meas.

Song No. 1
Dsichlyedje Hatal—Song from the Mountain Chant
(Navaho)

Natalie Curtis—Indians' Book, p. 408.

Arrow Dance of the Navaho

"This song," says Natalie Curtis (*The Indians' Book*, p. 362), "is an ancient Navaho war chant. It was sung by the god Nayenezrani, the Slayer of the Anaye. Nayenezrani made the ancient war-songs and gave them to the Navahos. In olden times, when the Navahos were going to war, the warriors chanted this song, and then went out into a wide plain, and put the war-feather in their hair. These feathers were very holy, and were ornamented with turquoise. No woman or child might ever look upon them, lest the warrior, in battle, become like a child or a woman.

"The war-chant tells how Nayenezrani hurls his enemies into the ground with the lightning, one after another. The four lightnings strike from him in all directions and return, for lightning always looks as if it flashed out and then went back."

The words of the chant follow, together with the translation which Miss Curtis gives:

Naye-e Sin	War-Song
Pesh ashike ni shli—yi-na, Pesh ashike ni shli—ya-e.	Lo, the flint youth, he am I; The flint youth.
Nayenezrani shi ni shli—kola Pesh ashike ni shli— E-na.	Nayenezrani, lo, behold me, he am I, Lo, the flint youth, he am I; The flint youth.
Pesh tilyilch-iye shi ke—kola, Pesh ashike ni shli— E-na.	Moccasins of black flint have I, Lo, the flint youth, he am I; The flint youth.
Pesh tilyilch-iye siskle—kola, Pesh ashike ni shli— E-na.	Leggings of black flint have I, Lo, the flint youth, he am I; The flint youth.
Pesh tilyilch-iye shi e—kola, Pesh ashike ni shli— E-na.	Tunic of black flint have I, Lo, the flint youth, he am I; The flint youth.

Song No. 2

Naye-e Sin—War Song (Navaho)

*Sing 5 times if using the words, but for dance only once.

Natalie Curtis—Indians' Book, p. 393.

Pesh tilyilch-iye shi tsha—kola,
  Pesh ashike ni shli—
      E-na.
	Bonnet of black flint have I,
	  Lo, the flint youth, he am I;
	      The flint youth.

Nolienni tshina shi-ye
Shi yiki holon-e—kola,
  Pesh ashike ni shli—
      E-na.
	Clearest, purest flint the heart
	Living strong within me—heart of flint;
	  Lo, the flint youth, he am I;
	      The flint youth.

Ka' itsiniklizhi-ye
  Din-ikwo
Sitzan nahatilch—kola,
  Din-ikwo
  Pesh ashike ni shli—
      E-na.
	Now the zigzag lightnings four
	      From me flash,
	Striking and returning,
	      From me flash;
	  Lo, the flint youth, he am I;
	      The flint youth.

Tsini nahatilch ki la
Nihoka hastoyo-la
Whe-e-yoni-s'n-iye
Yoya aiyinilch—kola,
  Pesh ashike ni shli—
      E-na.
	There where'er the lightnings strike,
	Into the ground they hurl the foe—
	Ancient folk with evil charms,
	One upon another, dashed to earth;
	  Lo, the flint youth, he am I;
	      The flint youth.

Ka' sa-a narai,
Ka' binihotsitti shi ni shli—kola,
  Pesh ashike ni shli—
      E-na.
	Living evermore,
	Feared of all forevermore,
	  Lo, the flint youth, he am I;
	      The flint youth.

Pesh ashike ni shli—kola, Pesh ashike ni shli—ya-e.	Lo, the flint youth, he am I; The flint youth.

The dance is a small section of the MOUNTAIN CHANT. In it, there are two dancers, men. In either hand they hold a zigzag arrow (Fig. 16), hung with long ribbons, and two eagle feathers in the middle.

FIG. 16.

Introduction   4 meas.

  (*a*) Shuffle in with very short steps, from opposite sides, toward
each other   11 meas.

  (*b*) Jump high in air, facing each other   1 meas.

  (*c*) Shuffle around each other, passing right shoulders   8 meas.

(*d*)	Hold, facing each other	1 meas.
(*e*)	With a very high trot step (2 steps to the measure), knees up in front at each step, but remaining in place	5 meas.
(*f*)	Jump high in air, ending back to back	1 meas.
(*g*)	High front-trot in place, back to back	13 meas.
(*h*)	Jump, ending side by side, facing front	1 meas.
(*i*)	Shuffle forward	5 meas.
(*j*)	Hold	1 meas.
(*k*)	Shuffle about each other, passing right shoulders	3 meas.
(*l*)	Hold, facing front	1 meas.
(*m*)	Shuffle about each other, passing left shoulders	8 meas.
(*n*)	Jump, ending facing each other, arrows high in air horizontally	1 meas.

Yei-Be-Chi

This is a most weird performance, as danced in the fire-light. It is part of the NIGHT CHANT, which, in its entirety, is a nine days' ceremony, and is given in order to cure any ill that springs from the lowlands or valleys.

There were twenty dancers, each with a rattle in the right hand. There was no drum, and the music was by the dancers themselves, rather yelped than sung. The music is here reproduced from Natalie Curtis' *Indians' Book* (p. 402); but the staccato yelping is impossible to be notated, and the melody is here much more pronounced than in reality.

(*a*) Enter, with back-trot step, in pairs, side by side   9 meas.

(*b*) Face front on the rest measure, bringing them into two sidewise lines, all facing front   1 meas.

(*c*) Feet perfectly still, but rattles shaken in time   2 meas.

(*d*) With a sudden, sharp bend of the knees, bow forward and yelp, straighten up, and face back   1 meas.

(*e*) Repeat (*c*) and (*d*), starting faces to back, then swinging to front again   3 meas.

(*f*) With the back-trot step, they melt into one line, facing front   4 meas.

(*g*) Repeat (*c*), (*d*), and (*e*)   6 meas.

(*h*) With back-trot step, they separate into two lines again, and the front line faces back   4 meas.

(*i*) The pair at the head of the group approach each other with the back-trot step; and side by side, go down between the two lines, then take their places at the end, each again in his own line. The second couple then come down the aisle in the same manner, then the third, etc. The group continue in place to shake their rattles and keep time with the back-trot step. Use as much music as it takes to give all a chance down the aisle.

Then in pairs with the back-trot step, they exeunt.

Song No. 3
Yei-be-chi Dance (Navaho)

Ha hol-la ha hol-la ha ha - ay Hol-la ho.... o hol-la
ho.. ha - ay Ho-a ha ha ho-a ha ho-a ha ha
Ha hol-la ha hol-la ho ha - ay Hol-la ho.... a hol-la
ho ha - ay Ho-a ha ha ho-a ha ho-a ha - ay

Natalie Curtis—The Indians' Book, p. 402.

Bow and Arrow Dance of Jemez

Eight dancers, each with bow in left hand, one arrow in right. Bells about waist; an apron of white embroidered as in CORN DANCE (see p. 152), red sash hanging down right side. Bare upper body; circle of white painted on breast. (Fig. 23.)

Instead of a drum, a hide was laid on the ground, before which the chorus kneeled, and beat in time. The rhythm was a fast, vigorous, three-part time, done loud-soft-rest; loud-soft-rest, etc.

The dance was made up of very definite figures, which I have combined as follows: (Use SONG OF THE PEACE PACT)

(*a*) Enter from left, one behind the other, with back-trot step (1 step to each count)   3 meas.

Then, 1 trot-step to first count of measure, then hold this position for the other 2 counts   1 meas.

(*b*) Repeat (*a*) in place   4 meas.

(*c*) Repeat (*a*) in place   4 meas.

(*d*) Face front, and shuffle to own left   4 meas.

Shuffle to own right   4 meas.

Shuffle about self   4 meas.

(In this, the two arms work simultaneously to left for one measure, to right for one measure, etc.)

(*e*) In circle, step right (1); hop right (2, 3), holding left foot in air   4 meas.

Reverse feet   4 meas.

Step right (1); hop right (2, 3) as above   2 meas.

Reverse feet   2 meas.

(*f*) Repeat step of (*e*), but in straight line, facing front, and progressing right and left   12 meas.

(*g*) Repeat again, but facing right, and progressing to right side   12 meas.

(*b*) 3 back-trot steps as in (*a*), in place   3 meas.

      About face, bend knees, and touch arrow to ground   1 meas.

      (On the turn and dip, the back foot taps twice.)

(*i*) Repeat, making the turn to front   4 meas.

      Repeat, making the turn to left side   4 meas.

(*j*) Back-trot step off   12 meas.

Song No. 4

Song of the Peace Pact (Chippewa)

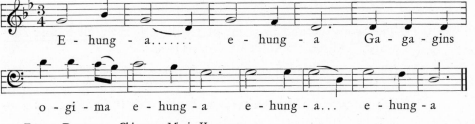

E - hung - a....... e - hung - a Ga - ga - gins

o - gi - ma e - hung - a e - hung - a... e - hung - a

Frances Densmore—Chippewa Music II, p. 127.

Basket Dance of Cochiti

Enter nine men in Corn Dance costume (see p. 152), rattles in right hand; nine women in Corn Dance costume, in one hand an inverted basket and a stick, in the other a spruce bough.

(*a*) The women stand in front of the line of men, all facing forward. All do the high back-trot step.

(*b*) The women face the men, kneel, place baskets on the ground, and go through the motions of grinding corn, in rhythm to the rattles of the men who violently tap the right foot forward in time.

(*c*) The women rise, face forward, and all repeat (*a*). (See Figs. 17 and 18.)

The BASKET DANCE is a fertility rite. Mary Austin, in her *American Rhythm*, has given the following as the translation of the song of the BASKET DANCE, made to her at San Ildefonso by a young man of the tribe:

"We, the Rain Cloud callers
Ancient mothers of the Rain Cloud clan,
Basket bearers;
We entreat you,
O ye Ancients,
By the full-shaped womb,
That the lightning and the thunder and the rain
Shall come upon the earth;
Shall fructify the earth;
That the great rain clouds shall come upon the earth
As the lover to the maid.

"Send your breath to blow the clouds,
O ye Ancients,
As the wind blows the plumes
Of our eagle-feathered prayer sticks,
Send, O ye Ancients,
To the six Corn Maidens.
To the White Corn Maiden,
To the Yellow Corn Maiden,
To the Red Corn Maiden,

38

To the Blue Corn Maiden,
To the Many Colored Maiden,
To the Black Corn Maiden,
That their wombs bear fruit.

"Let the thunder be heard,
O ye Ancients!
Let the sky be covered with white blossom clouds,
That the earth, O ye Ancients,
Be covered with many colored flowers.
That the seeds come up,
That the stalks grow strong,
That the people have corn,
That happily they eat.
Let the people have corn to complete the road of life."

Basket Dance of Woodcraft

As music for this dance, I have used THE DUST OF THE RED WAGON, though it is not of the Cochiti tribe.

Enter six men, wearing breech clouts and headbands. Each carries in his right hand a gourd rattle, in his left a prayer plume (see Fig. 66), held high in the air. With back-trot step, go once around circle, softly shaking rattles, and chanting song   8 meas.

Line up, facing front, and vigorously tap right foot forward in time, and continue this while the maidens make their entrance   6 meas.

Enter six Corn Maidens, dressed simply, and alike except for *tablitas* (headdresses) which are of different colors—one white, one yellow, one red, one blue, one black, and one spotted in various colors, symbolizing the different colors of the corn grown in the Southwest. Each carries a flat round basket under the right arm. They use the women's step (No. 39), progressing sidewise until they are lined up in front of the men, also facing front   8 meas.

Now the maidens change to the tap step that the men are using, but do not raise the right foot as high on each tap as do the men   6 meas.

The maidens now grasp the baskets in both hands, flat side forward. In time to the music (up and down to each measure), they raise and lower the baskets from full arms' length to the waistline   4 meas.

Face right, and continue the same arm movement   4 meas.

Face front, and continue the same arm movement   2 meas.

Face left, and continue the same arm movement   2 meas.

Face the men, and continue the same arm movement   2 meas.

The maidens kneel before the men (who are still tapping in place), and put baskets on the ground in front of them   2 meas.

They squat back, hands clasped in front on laps   2 meas.

The men wave their prayer plumes over the baskets   2 meas.

The men shake their rattles over the baskets   2 meas.

FIG. 17.—THE BASKET DANCE
FIG. 19.—THE COMANCHE DANCE

FIG. 18.—THE BASKET DANCE
FIG. 20.—THE JOY DANCE

With back-trot step, each man encircles the maiden before him, still shaking the rattle over her head   3 meas.

When he is back in his place, he drops his right hand low, though still shaking the rattle, and waves his prayer plume over the maiden   3 meas.

The maidens pick up the baskets in both hands, holding them flat side up, as if offering them to the men   2 meas.

The men shake the rattles high over the baskets   2 meas.

The men again encircle the maidens, shaking their rattles over them   2 meas.

When they are back in their places, the maidens rise, hold the baskets high in air   2 meas.

The maidens pivot to right, 1½ turns, so as to end facing front   6 meas.

All tap-step again in place   4 meas.

The men now take steps forward, until they are in one line with the maidens, each to the right of his own maiden   4 meas.

With the back-trot step, all make one circle, and exeunt   6 meas.

Song No. 5

The Dust of the Red Wagon (Ute)

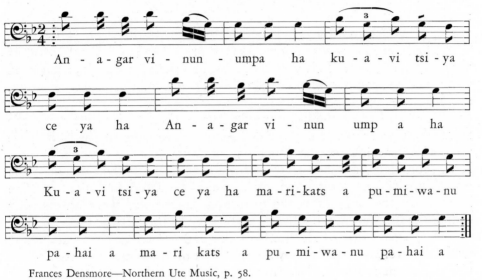

An - a - gar vi - nun - umpa ha ku - a - vi tsi - ya

ce ya ha An - a - gar vi - nun ump a ha

Ku - a - vi tsi - ya ce ya ha ma - ri - kats a pu - mi - wa - nu

pa - hai a ma - ri kats a pu - mi - wa - nu pa - hai a

Frances Densmore—Northern Ute Music, p. 58.

Pipe Dance of San Juan

I cannot reproduce the music which was used for this dance; but give that of a PIPE DANCE of the Chippewa, recorded by Frances Densmore (*Chippewa Music*, II, p. 294). Of the PIPE DANCE among these tribes, Miss Densmore says:

"The Pipe Dance was said to be the principal 'good time dance' of the early Chippewa. It is very old; and, like all other dances, is believed to have come from the *manido*. In this dance, a man carried a pipestem, and his body was supposed to represent a pipe. The dancer never rose erect, but took a crouching or squatting posture, trying to assume the form of a pipe as nearly as possible. Many contortions of the body were used, and the antics of the dancers were considered very amusing. . . . It was considered a test of courage for a man to brave the ridicule of the assembly, and seat himself where he would be asked to dance the Pipe Dance. In the early days, the men who danced this wore no clothing except the moccasins, which were a necessity to protect the feet.

"A characteristic of the music of this dance is that a sharp short beat of the drum is frequently given, followed by an instant of silence. When this drumbeat is heard, the dancer pauses in whatever attitude he may chance to be, and remains motionless until the drumbeat is resumed." This pause is indicated in the music by the rest in each of the ¾ time measures, and is a characteristic of much of the music and dancing of the Southwest.

The dance is a prayer for the rain clouds to form.

It is performed by two dancers.

(*a*) Holding a pipe at waist level in both hands, they bend the body forward at each two steps, and backward at each two, enter with the back-trot step (2 steps to each measure)   8 meas.

(*b*) Stand perfectly still while the chorus continues the song   4 meas.

At the second and fourth of these four measures, the dancers bend both knees quickly, and yelp once.

(*c*) Trot right, left, hold   1 meas.

(*d*) Drop foot, and bend knees, giving one yelp   1 meas.

(e) With back-trot step in place, and bending body as in (a), but holding pipes up at arms' length and looking up at them 4 meas.

(f) Trot, trot, hold 1 meas.

(g) Drop foot, bend knees, and yelp 1 meas.

(h) Quickly about face, and repeat whole in opposite direction.

Song No. 6

Ogima—Chippewa Pipe Dance Song

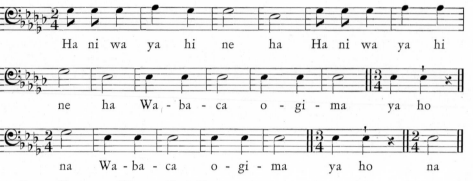

Ha ni wa ya hi ne ha Ha ni wa ya hi

ne ha Wa - ba - ca o - gi - ma ya ho

na Wa - ba - ca o - gi - ma ya ho na

Frances Densmore—Chippewa Music II, p. 294.

Dog Dance of San Juan

Two male dancers, nude except for white apron, embroidered in colors; beaded moccasins; bells below knees; wide armlet above elbow hung with ribbons; Sioux war bonnet with long tail of eagle feathers. Each carries a red oblong about 12 inches wide and 6 inches high, attached at top to a stick, horizontally; feathers hanging from bottom of oblong. This is held in the left hand by the stick, so as to hide the face. Each carries a rattle in the right hand. A long red knitted woman's belt attached at back of waistline, one woman holding the two other ends. The woman wears the conventional black dress, and square white shawl edged with a broad band of red.

The Dogs dance very much bent forward. The two steps they use are:

(*a*) Single step around selves. Each time they face the woman, she bends knees in curtsey.

(*b*) As (*a*), but double time, the woman shuffling.

The Dogs dance in absolute unison, facing the same direction all the time, going round and round themselves.

I do not know whether the Pueblos have a story of the Dog Feast parallel to that of the Dakota. But there are elements in the above dance which suggest such a probability.

The story told by Chief Maza-Blaska is as follows:

"Behold, it was thus: Once, long ago, in the season of falling leaves, the Dakotas went hunting at the edge of the Black Hills. The people were starving, and great was their need of meat. So they vowed: 'If only we find buffalo, we will give all our dogs a feast.' This they vowed.

"Lo, soon afterwards they saw a herd and killed many buffaloes, and came back to their camp, weary but rejoicing. Then, true to their vow, they made a great feast for their dogs; in the centre of the camp, they piled all the tallow from the buffaloes, and amid this they scattered the tongues. So they did, giving to the dogs the choicest morsels. Then the men took their dogs and painted them for the feast. With a stripe of red down the back, and red on the side of the jaw, they painted them.

"Then they led them to the pile of tallow in the centre of the camp, and held them in a circle while all sang, 'May you feast well, O dog!'

47

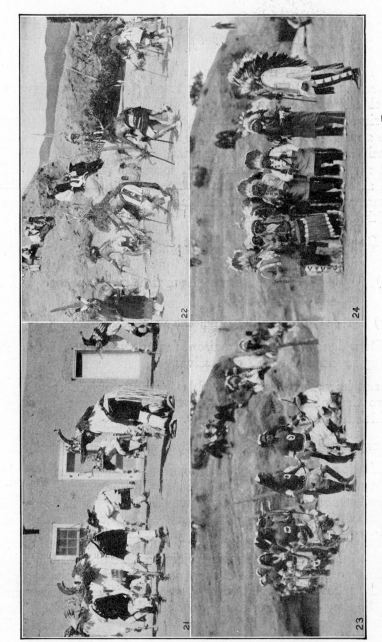

FIG. 21.—THE DEER DANCE
FIG. 23.—THE BOW AND ARROW DANCE

FIG. 22.—THE BUFFALO DANCE
FIG. 24.—A TYPICAL CHORUS

Three times they sang this song, while the dogs strained and growled and yelped. Then a man cried out, 'Hold well your dogs. Once more shall the song be sung.'

"So yet again the people sang, while the dogs strained harder; then at the last of the song—away! The dogs flew at the meat, and devoured it eagerly, every morsel. Lo, they as well as their masters had hungered long." (*Indians' Book*, p. 58.)

Out of this story and the song that goes with it, and with pictures in mind of the San Juan Dog Dance, we suggest:

Song No. 7

Shunka Olowan—Song of the Dog Feast (Sioux)

Shun - ka wa - ya - a - a - ta - ni - i - i - in Shun - ka wa -

ya - a - a - ta - ni - i - i - in Shun - ka - wa - ya - a - a - ta -

ni - i - i - in Shun - ka wa - ya - a - a - ta - ni - i - i - in

Shun - ka wa - ya - a - a - ta - ni - i - i - in Shun - ka wa -

ya - a - a - ta - ni - i - i - in e - ya e - e yo

Natalie Curtis—Indians' Book, p. 88.

Dog Dance of Woodcraft

(*a*) Enter, from all possible corners, singing, pairs of dancers—in each pair, one representing the Dog, dressed as above; and behind him, the Master, holding him by the leash. The war bonnet shows that the Dogs are the ones to be honored; and the red oblongs hide the faces, acting as masks and disguising the character. The Dogs are straining at the leashes; the Masters holding them back. Use one step to each measure; but be accurate in the changes of rhythm from 3-part to 2-part time. On the last measure, the Dogs yelp twice 5 meas.

(*b*) Still straining, Masters trot-step sidewise to left, pulling the Dogs, the latter yelping again on the last measure   5 meas.

(*c*) The Masters trot-step in toward center, the Dogs to their left toward outside of circle, exchanging places   5 meas.

(*d*) The Masters strain back, the Dogs paw the ground with right foot, bodies bent forward at waist   5 meas.

(*e*) All trot-step to right, Dogs diagonally in front of Masters, in an outer circle, and barking   5 meas.

(*f*) Dogs cross in front of Masters, trot-step in toward center, and drop to all-fours in a small circle   5 meas.

(*g*) The Masters drop leashes, stand in outer circle, feet tight together; both hands at sides, a little backward, palms forward; head bowed, and sing last 6 measures of song, while Dogs drop heads to ground in front of knees, chanting Ah-ooooo Ah-oooooo Ah-ooooooo   6 meas.

Deer Dance of San Juan

This is a dance calling upon the Deer to increase, and to choose nearby stamping grounds.

On February 26, 1930, I saw a beautiful presentation of this dance at the pueblo of San Juan, New Mexico.

At dawn, the eighteen Deer came running in from the high mountain about a mile back of the pueblo. They wore ordinary White man's shirts, with armbands above each elbow, some solidly beaded, some of painted buckskin, each holding in place close to the outside of the arm, a branch of evergreen. The hands were painted white. The trousers were tight-fitting to the leg, crocheted of white cotton in an openwork zigzag pattern running up and down. Over these, hanging almost to the knees, each wore a white woven apron, embroidered in colors at the ends, open down the back; a white sash with long fringe, at the top of which was a row of large white covered balls; a string of bells about the waist; below each knee a garter tied in front with a long hank of colored worsted; gay colored ties about the neck loosely knotted, and many strings of beads; colored moccasins, most of them beaded, Sioux fashion, and all with a band of black skunk skin around the top.

In the right hand each carried a gourd rattle; in the left, a wand, head-high, surmounted by three feathers, the two outer ones eagle feathers, and the inner, a beautifully colored macaw or similar. These three feathers were held in place, together with a sprig of evergreen, by a white cone about four inches high. Halfway down, the wand was wound with colored cotton and a little fluff.

The headdresses were very beautiful. They were of yellow yucca stalks, each stalk about a half inch in thickness, woven close together into an upright fan, with a two-inch wide band of green painted across it three inches from the top. This arc was attached to a fabric cap, which carried also a pair of muledeer horns, tipped with gray down. The cap was tied under the chin to keep it in place. Down the back, at the shoulders, hung a half-circle of eagle feathers, tips down. The cloth which carried these, was tucked into the back of the belt. The back of the neck was painted white. (See Fig. 25.)

These eighteen Deer were headed by an old Medicine Man, with a wonderfully beautiful face. His long hair hung in soft waves to his waist, and was topped by two eagle feathers. He wore a pair of Sioux pants, beaded down the outer seams, an ordinary shirt, and moccasins. There was a peculiar box-like arrangement tied to the back of his belt, hung

52

Deer Dancer,
by Crisenzio Roybar
of San Ildefonso

FIG. 25.

with yellow buckskin. He carried a large bunch of evergreen in his right hand, with which he directed the rhythm of the dance.

Before the approach of the Deer at dawn, there had been planted in the plaza two small evergreen trees, each about three feet high, and some thirty feet apart. The whole dance took place in a straight line between these two trees.

The Deer, one behind the other, trot-step in place to the rhythm of the song they sing, and the thumping of the one tombé. There were no words to the song, scarcely even vocables; it was a peculiar propulsion of sound in a faintly melodious air.

The long wands were held obliquely in front of each dancer by the left hand, and never left the ground during the rendition of the song; until all about-faced and repeated the music and dance in the opposite direction. The Medicine Man slowly moved with his step along the line of the dancers, always facing forward.

When the dance was about half finished, there appeared two hunters, their faces painted white and black, and dressed more or less in the manner of clowns. One wore a wide band of black fur about the forehead, with an eagle wing over each ear; the other a stockinette cap of gray, with black and white turkey feathers in a bunch at the top. Each carried a bow, and wore a quiver of arrows (really reeds). These hunters manœuvred about, and occasionally shot one of the arrows over the head of some Deer, lightly touching the headdress of the victim.

This went on for some twenty minutes, and was repeated after a rest period.

Toward the end of the afternoon, after a pause in the dancing during which they sang in one of the houses, the dancers reappeared, each now with a short stick, about eighteen inches long, in each hand, body bent forward over these as if walking on all fours.

Suddenly, they rose up and ran, followed by the women of the pueblo. We could see them for half a mile across the desert. When caught, all returned to the pueblo. The Deer must give the woman who caught him some meat; the woman gives the Deer some flour.

Meantime, the four Deer who had been shot by the hunters, kneeled down in one place, and were addressed in loud harangue by the hunters. This was their official execution.

Deer Dance of the Navahos

This is an original dance, suggested by the HUNTING SONG (*Dinni-e Sin*), recorded by Natalie Curtis in her *Indians' Book*, p. 369.

"All animals of the chase are the herds of Hastyeyalti, God of Sunrise. He is god of game, and he made the hunting songs and gave them to the Navahos. In the old days, before they were shepherds, the Navahos lived by hunting. The Navaho hunter sits quite still and chants a song, and the game comes straight to him. When the animal is near enough, the hunter shoots him through the heart. The Navahos say that the deer like the song of the hunter, and come from all directions to hear it. . . . This can be readily believed, for the Indian can be absolutely immovable. The measured chant attracts the animals, who, always curious, first come to find out what the sound is, and are then almost hypnotised, as it were, by the monotony and rhythm of the chanting. . . . Pueblo Indians say that before they start on the hunt, they sing, bending every thought on prayerful wish for success. While they sing, the distant deer gather in council, and choose to whom each will fall. To those who have been most devout in singing will the animals go. This idea is held by the Navahos also, as is shown in this song. Indians believe in man's power to draw to himself or to bring about that upon which he fixes his mind in song and prayer. . . .

"In this song, the hunter likens himself to the beautiful blackbird loved by the deer. The Navahos say that this bird alights on the animals, and sometimes tries to make its nest between the horns. The refrain of the song tells of the coming of the deer—how he makes a trail from the top of Black Mountain down through the fair meadows, how he comes through the dewdrops and the pollen of the flowers, and then how, startled at sight of the hunter, he stamps and turns to run. But the man kills him, and will kill yet many another, for he is lucky and blessed in hunting. The Navahos say that the male deer always starts with the left foreleg, the female with the right.

"This is an ancient song made by the god Hastyeyalti:

"*Hunting Song*

"Comes the deer to my singing,
Comes the deer to my song,
Comes the deer to my singing.

55

"He, the blackbird, he am I,
Bird beloved of the wild deer.
Comes the deer to my singing.

"From the Mountain Black,
From the summit,
Down the trail, coming, coming now,
Comes the deer to my singing.

"Through the blossoms,
Through the flowers, coming, coming now,
Comes the deer to my singing.

"Through the flower dewdrops,
Coming, coming now,
Comes the deer to my singing.

"Through the pollen, flower pollen,
Coming, coming now,
Comes the deer to my singing.

"Starting with his left forefoot,
Stamping, turns the frightened deer,
Comes the deer to my singing.

"Quarry mine, blessed am I
In the luck of the chase.
Comes the deer to my singing.

"Comes the deer to my singing,
Comes the deer to my song,
Comes the deer to my singing."

The Dance

This may be a duo or a group dance. I shall describe it as done by a group of four.

(*a*) Introduction   1 meas.

(From this point, the hunters should chant the song.)

(*b*) Enter, from right, with back-trot step 4 hunters, each carrying a bow and arrow high in left hand. For this back-trot step, the left foot is raised very little at the back and takes but one count; the right is raised much higher and held for 2 counts   4 meas.

(c) With same step, done in place, facing left in a straight line, holding bows down at sides   2 meas.

(d) Face front, and continue same step in place, holding bows in front   2 meas.

(e) Face right, and continue step in place, bows down at side   2 meas.

(f) Face front, and with feet still, both hands upraised to Great Spirit, sing   4 meas.

(g) The hunter who was the first to enter, trots to front left corner, and there continues to mark time   1 meas.

(h) The hunter who was the last to enter, does the same to the front right corner   1 meas.

(i) The second and third hunters make for the back left and back right corners respectively, both going at the same time   1 meas.

(j) The hunters sit each in his corner, bow laid across his lap, arms folded on his breast, and sing   5 meas.

(k) Enter 4 deer, using step No. 20. They wear each a headdress of yucca stems from temple to temple, with antlers shooting up from the middle of each. They have a cane in either hand, used as the forefeet. They cautiously make one round of the circle   9 meas.

(l) The hunters continue the singing. The deer stand in listening attitude, turning heads from side to side   4 meas.

(m) The deer turn about slowly, so each faces a hunter. The hunters, still singing, rise on one knee, and aim with their bows   2 meas.

(n) The deer approach, each his own hunter, until they are quite close, face to face   2 meas.

(o) With sneak step, each hunter surrounds his deer, the latter turning so as to always face the hunter, hypnotized   3 meas.

(p) All stand still, each pair facing. The hunter lets fly his arrow (imaginary). The deer fall to the ground   2 meas.

(q) The hunters raise both hands to the Great Spirit, singing   2 meas.

(r) With step-drag-close (No. 1), each hunter surrounds his deer   2 meas.

(s) With Sioux hop-step (No. 26), each hunter exits at his own corner   2 meas.

Song No. 8

Dinni-e Sin—Hunting Song (Navaho)

tra - a.. shte.. lo Ye sha - kai... ka-tal i ne ye yan ga
Din - ni - tsche-be- kan i ye Bi - tzil - le Desh - kla - ash dji... lo
Ye sha kai... ka-tal i ne ye yan ga Bi - se - dje
ka' shi - ye - no sin - e.. ku... lo Ye sha - kai... ka-tal
i ne ye yan ga ye sha-kai... ka-tal ai... ye... lo
Ye sha - kai... ka-tal i ne ya Ye sha - kai.. ka-tal
ai.. ye... lo Ye sha - kai.. ka-tal - i - ne - ya

Natalie Curtis—Indians' Book, p. 413.

Eagle Dance of Tesuque

At Tesuque (Indian, *Te-tsu-ge*, the cottonwood place), they are said to have the best Eagle dancers. One of these was Martin Vigil. The Indians consider the eagle the connecting link between Heaven and Earth; the eagle plumes are the prayer bearers.

Alice Corbin Henderson has said of this dance (*Theatre Arts Magazine*, April, 1923, p. 110): "The Eagle Dance, performed by the San Ildefonso or the Tesuque Pueblo, has all the delicacy and finesse of Pavlova's Dance of the Swan."

The chorus in the performance which we saw was composed of five men—four wearing Sioux war bonnets, and the center one a bright colored silk head hankie. They were clad in White men's shirts, long trousers decorated down the outside seams, beaded moccasins, and armlets. Some wore colored blankets draped around their middles. Two carried war drums (tombés); all sang. Victor record 20043 gives this song, of which I have tried to notate a characteristic portion (Song No. 9).

There were, as always, two Eagle dancers. They were painted yellow on their bare forelegs and breast. The upper legs were painted white, and the rest of the body dark blue. Around the edge of the yellow breast were fastened soft, short white feathers. Each wore a short white skirt, embroidered in colors; bells about the waistline; red garters, fringed, below the knee where the yellow legs joined the white. The close-fitting wig or cap was made of short white feathers, with a yellow bill attached. The wings were a strip of yellow material, extending across at back of the neck, along the arm line, farther than the fingertips. To the back side of this were fastened the long eagle plumes hanging in a straight line. Each wore a dancing bustle as tail. They were barefooted. (See Figs. 26 and 27.)

FIGS. 26, 27.—THE EAGLE DANCE AT TESUQUE

Eagle Dance of Woodcraft

Enter one Eagle dancer, costumed as per foregoing description, body bent forward, swinging wings from side to side, with a slow, simple walk (1 step and swing to each measure). Thus he makes one circuit of the dancing space   14 meas.

As he passes the entrance on the beginning of his second round, enter the other Eagle, as above, but progresses in opposite direction. The first Eagle has changed his step to step forward right, step forward left with a low dip   7 meas.

They meet at one side of the circle, hesitate with both wing tips meeting overhead, facing each other   3 meas.

They cautiously encircle each other, lowering the wings and raising them again   4 meas.

Then each completes his own circle to opposite side of the center   7 meas.

Face to face again, they hesitate, waving arms, and bending knees well   3 meas.

With feet close together, they hop, hop, hop, each to his own right flapping the wings menacingly   1 meas.

To his own left   1 meas.

To right   1 meas.

To left   1 meas.

More calmly, they again encircle each other   4 meas.

As No. 1 again starts to make the circle, No. 2 hesitates   4 meas.

No. 2 turns, and follows No. 1   6 meas.

After another round, one behind the other, they step side by side   7 meas.

With the high hop-point step, they progress to right   1 meas.

To left, forward, and back (1 meas. each) working in perfect unison   3 meas.

Now they face each other   3 meas.

Softly sway the wings parallel to each other   4 meas.

With the step and dip, they go off together, wings overlapping   10 meas.

Song No. 9
Eagle Dance

Notated by Julia M. Buttree from Victor Record 20043.

Hoop Dance of Taos

We saw the HOOP DANCE OF TAOS twice—once at Taos as a solo by Juanito Lujan, the son of the governor; and once at the Gallup Ceremonial as a group dance. We saw two hoop dancers also at Standing Rock, North Dakota (see Fig. 28), one with a flexible hoop covered with down or short feathers.

FIG. 28.—HOOP DANCER AT STANDING ROCK

The costuming at Taos was very simple: bare body, except for colored neckerchief; breech clout of apron shape, front and back, split up both sides; string of bells just below each knee; and moccasins. He wore a beaded handband, and carried a hoop about two feet in diameter.

In the group presentation, they wore short black velvet pants, yellow shirts, and one a dancing bustle.

At Standing Rock, they wore all the clothes they could muster.

The time of the music was a fast 1-2, 1-2, accented on the 1.

The steps which they used, we have combined and organized into the following routine:

Woodcraft Hoop Dance

We use four dancers, each carrying a hoop wrapped with white table oilcloth (to make it more visible at night in the firelight); and costumed in breech clouts, if boys. If girls, as follows:

A pair of short, brown, tight-fitting pants, a sleeveless straight-cut waist of same material, tucked into the waist of the pants so as to make an unbroken line, the whole zigzagged in white paint from shoulder to bottom of pants, or even running right down leg to ankle. This necessitates some make-up to get the warm brown color, and we aim to have the make-up and the material of the costume of the same color. Around the waist, a brilliant-colored breech clout, shaped as in Fig. 88 and weighted at the tabs. These may be decorated in any fashion desired. Bells are worn around the leg under the knee, or small tinkles down the outside seam of the pants; but it is better not to have them around the ankle as in other dances, since it is likely to interfere with hoop work at times.

(*a*) GERONIMO'S MEDICINE SONG, Section I:
Skip in (9 steps), one dancer from each of the four corners, and swinging the hoops out and up right, down into left

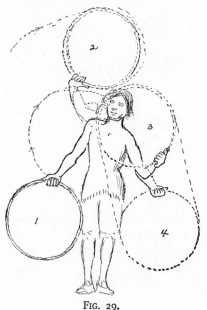

FIG. 29.

65

hand, out and up left, down into right hand, etc., forming figures-of-8 in the air (Fig. 29). Meet in center, facing in
9 meas.

(b) Section II:
All face left. Five step-hops in circle, swinging hoops back with right hand around middle, into left hand and across waistline into right hand, etc. This step-hop is always done with a slight bend forward at waist, unless otherwise specified
5 meas.

(c) Section III:
About face. Eight step-hops as in (b), ending with pose (1 meas.), all facing center, holding hoops up in right hand in the vertical plane, and with circles to center
9 meas.

(d) Section IV:
Face left. Step right toe forward (1); left heel tap, tap (2&1&); drop right heel (2); repeat on opposite foot, and repeat whole to end of strain
10 meas.

(e) Section V:
Repeat (d)
9 meas.

(f) Section V repeated:
Sixteen back-trot steps, raising heels high behind (2 steps to each measure), and ending with pose (1 measure), all facing

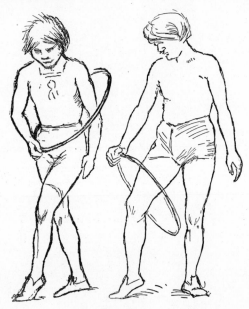

FIG. 30.

center, holding hoops high in front with both hands, hoops in horizontal plane   9 meas.

(*g*) APACHE MEDICINE SONG:

Facing center, hoop down at right side in right hand, toe-flat step right foot to right (1&); cross left in front of right (2&); step right into hoop (1&); step left into hoop (2&); swing hoop up left over head (1&); and down to right side again (2&). Repeat until last line   12 meas.

With same step, all string out into one line, next each other, facing front (Fig. 30)   4 meas.

(*h*) GERONIMO'S MEDICINE SONG, Section I:

Hang hoop low in front across the body with right hand. Hop-step right into hoop, repeat (1&2&); hop-step right out of hoop back in place, repeat (1&2&); hop-step left into hoop, repeat (1&2&); hop-step left out of hoop back in place, repeat (1&2&); hop-step right into hoop, crossing

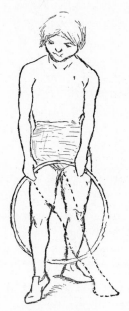

FIG. 31.

front of left (1&); hop-step right still in hoop, but not crossing left (2&); hop-step right into hoop, crossing front of left (1&); hop-step right out of hoop (2&); hop-step left into hoop, crossing front of right, (1&); hop-step left still in hoop, but not crossing right (2&); hop-step left into hoop, crossing front of right (1&); hop-step left out of hoop (2&). (See Fig. 31)   9 meas.

(i) Section I, repeated:

Face left, and repeat *(h)*, one behind the other   9 meas.

(j) Section II, twice:

About face to right, spacing out into circle again. Hop-step back with right (1&); hop-step back with left (2&); hop-step back with right into hoop held at back of heels (1&); ditto with left (2&); swing hoop up front and over head (1&); swing hoop down back (2&). Repeat to end of strain (Fig. 32)   5 meas.

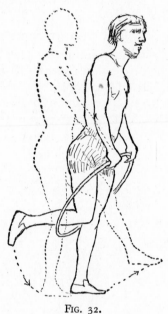

FIG. 32.

(k) Section III:

About face. Simple hop-step forward in circle, each passing own hoop back with right hand, hoop taken by next dancer with left hand, passed back and taken in right, etc.   9 meas.

(l) Section IV:

Face center, extend left leg back, hoop held over head 2 meas.
In 4 jerks, lower hoops to floor, and leave them there, all touching in center   2 meas.
Stand   1 meas.
Pivot to right, making one and a half turns, ending facing right   3 meas.
Pose, right hand up over head   2 meas.

(m) Section V:

Face right. Hop left, and cross right over left into hoop (1&); hop right and cross left outside of hoop (2&); pro-

68

gressing forward so the next hop-cross brings right into next hoop, and so on through the strain. At last measure, stoop quickly and pick up hoop   9 meas.

(*n*)   APACHE MEDICINE SONG:

About face to left. Lift left leg and put it through hoop held high as possible. Pass left arm through, then head. Swing hoop down back, and step right leg out of it. Swing hoop around middle once. (Fig. 33.) Repeat to end of strain, ending facing center, with hoops held in both hands back of heads   16 meas.

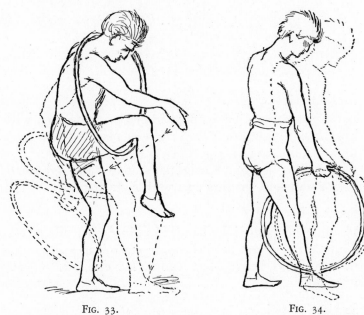

FIG. 33.   FIG. 34.

(*o*)   Cross left over right, and point (1&); then back to place (2&); cross right over left, and point (1&); then back to place (2&), etc. This is a rest step   9 meas.

(*p*)   Section I of GERONIMO's MEDICINE SONG:

Face left. Lower hoop to vertical plane, almost touching floor between feet. Hop left, step right across into hoop (1&); hop right, step left across into hoop in front of right (2&); hop left, bring right out (1&); hop right, and bring left out (2&); repeat to end of strain (Fig. 34)   9 meas.

(*q*)   Section II, twice:

About face to right. Swinging hoop behind, and holding it in both hands, bending sharply forward at waist, hop-step back, hop-step back, pass body through hoop, then head and feet, swing hoop down around to back, and repeat whole to end of strain (Fig. 35)   8 meas.

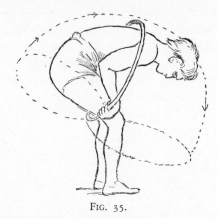

FIG. 35.

(r) Section III:

Backs to center. Take hoops in circle. Hop left, with right knee raised high, point-step right in place. Repeat for three lines, progressing to right   6 meas.

On last line, let go of neighbor's hoop with right hand, and turn about self, shading eyes with right hand   3 meas.

(s) Section IV:

Holding hoop in right hand, high in front, put left leg into hoop, left arm and head through, grasp it in left hand, change to right hand, leaving left leg in. Reverse, and repeat to end of strain   10 meas.

(t) Section V, twice:

One dancer stands in circle, hoop high over head; one at either side, facing each other; and one behind, facing front. The side dancers place their hoops vertically in front of selves so they overlap a little in front of center dancer. Center dancer steps into intersection of the two hoops which are immediately raised to waistline and pulled taut in horizontal plane. The dancer behind quickly puts own hoop over center dancer's head, and pulls taut at waist. (Center dancer must manage own hoop from hand to hand, so it does not interfere with this last movement.) Center dancer now pivots in place; other three hop-step around in small circle, each holding own hoop. At end of strain, all three outside dancers bend, holding hoops flat on ground   8 meas.

Center dancer leaps out   1 meas.

Center dancer leads off in rapid trot-step, other three following   9 meas.

This may be simplified by omitting any number of steps; may also be used as a solo by choosing the fitting steps.

Song No. 10
Geronimo's Medicine Song (Apache)

Natalie Curtis—The Indians' Book, pp. 325-26.

Song No. 11

Apache Medicine Song

Comanche Dance of Zuni

We saw three dances named as above. Two of them were so nearly alike that I combine my notes on them. The third was so totally different that I shall describe it separately as SECOND COMANCHE DANCE OF ZUNI.

It is said that the Zunis, during the early Indian wars, danced this to torment and irritate the Comanches.

There was an orchestra of four men, wearing Sioux war bonnets, each with a big drum.

Enter thirteen women, dressed as in CORN DANCE, but without the evergreens, and each bearing a large decorated pot on her head. They formed a half-circle at back, and did not dance.

To fast single beat, enter six dancers. Bodies nude, except for bright colored breech clouts in apron effect almost to ankles front and back; and wads of cotton-wool pasted all over the body. A feather in either hand. (See Fig. 19.)

Each did any step at any time, regardless of the others, but in strict rhythm, and keeping the general line of the dance in a zigzag.

The principal steps were:

(a) Very low bent, heel and toe step. At end of each phrase of the song, straighten up, then repeat

(b) Low bent, and shading eyes with one hand, pivot, one foot still, other pushing with short, sharp steps

(c) Two feet close together and worked simultaneously, hop to right, right, right; or left, left, left; or forward, forward, forward; knees much bent

(d) Suddenly end any of the above steps in a charge position, and hold it for several counts

Much tossing of the head from side to side throughout

Exit, followed by the pot-bearers

For those who wish a definitely planned dance corresponding to this, we might suggest using the song of CAROUSAL for the following routine:

Song No. 12
Carousal (Ojibway)

Kah nin-dah-ne-bah seneen kah nin-dah-ne-bah
se-neen ke tah-go-go-bah gaun-je nan-ka ma min
ne-quay aung kah nin-dah-ne-bah se-neen

Frederick R. Burton—American Primitive Music, p. 226.

Comanche Dance of Woodcraft

I

Enter with back-trot step (1 count to each step), closing into a circle   15 meas.

II

With body much bent forward at hips, heel-toe step right, left (1 measure to each foot)   2 meas.

Heel-toe step right, straightening body with sudden movement   1 meas.

Repeat these two movements, alternating the feet   12 meas.

III

(a) Body low bent, and shading eyes with right hand, looking about sharply, pivot in place   3 meas.

(b) Straighten body, hands on hips, two feet close together and worked simultaneously, hop forward, forward, forward (6 times in all, twice to each measure)   3 meas.

(c) Repeat (a)   3 meas.

(d) Repeat (b), but hopping backward instead of forward   3 meas.

(e) Charge forward   3 meas.

IV

Exit, using back-trot step   15 meas.

Song No. 13

Song of Rising to Depart (Osage)

A - ki-pa win-da-do   ho - pe-dse ton tha   A - ki-pa win-da-do

ho - pe - dse ton tha   A - ki - pa win - da - do   ho - pe-dse ton tha

Francis La Flesche—39th Ann. Rep. Bur. Eth., p. 237. Music transcribed by A. C. Fletcher.

Second Comanche Dance of the Zunis

A chorus of men, as in the preceding description; also the background of women.

The dancers were two men, four women, and one impersonated Coyote.

The women dancers wore red skirts, turquoise-blue waists, buckskin shirts like men's, fringed. The men dressed as in the preceding dance. The Coyote wears a headdress like the head of a Coyote.

The entrance was in a straight line—a man, four women, a man; the Coyote followed and capered about in all directions, doing any step so long as it was in rhythm.

Throughout the dance, frequent yelps by the dancers.

There were two principal steps, which I have used in the following routine.

The music is not what was used on that occasion, but carries the dance.

Coyote Dance of Woodcraft

(*a*) Enter, in a straight line, from right, with back-trot step, lifting feet backward very fast, and the right foot much higher than the left (4 steps to each measure)   4 meas.

(*b*) Stop, all facing left; repeat (*a*)   4 meas.

(*c*) Face front. The four women remain in place, doing the same step, but not so much lift to the feet. The Coyote stands in front of the line and changes his step to:—Limp forward right (1); close with left (&); limp forward right (2); close with left (&); limp forward right (1); close with left (&); charge forward right (2&). Repeat, starting with other foot. The men, in a straight line from their places, progress forward at either side of the Coyote   8 meas.

(*d*) The men stand where this has carried them, and switch to the back-trot step; while the Coyote returns to position in front of the women, using any step he likes, as long as it is in rhythm   8 meas.

(*e*) Now he repeats (*c*), followed by the women, until the latter are again in a straight line with the men   8 meas.

(*f*) All now back-trot together in place   4 meas.

(*g*) All face right, and back-trot off, led by the Coyote   4 meas.

Harvest Dance of Zuni

For this dance, there was an orchestra of men, dressed in their ordinary garb, with bright-colored head handkerchiefs, sashes, etc., over more or less White man's clothes. There were two war drums (tombés), accompanied by the voices of all.

Enter thirteen women, in Corn Dance costumes (see p. 151), but without the evergreens, and bearing each a large decorated Zuni pot on her head. They formed a shallow semi-circle at the back, but did not dance.

Enter the dancers, men and women, the former with bows and arrows.

The dance was nothing more than a rapid back-trot step, in vigorous four-part time.

It is a dance of thanksgiving for the gathered crops.

This might be worked into a story as follows:

Bow and Arrow Dance of Woodcraft

Enter the Chief, followed by as many Medicine Men as desired. All sit about the fire in a circle, smoking, except the Chief, who, standing and in silence, holds up his pipe to the Great Spirit; then addresses the Medicine Men:

"My friends, we have come again through a time of trial, a time of hunger, a time of want. For many suns, there was no meat in the pueblo, for many suns the babies cried for food."

First Medicine Man: "Yea, Chief, death walked with my little Tawak."

Second Medicine Man: "Oh, Chief, the Great Spirit called my woman."

Chief: "Yea, my friends, our hearts were troubled. . . . Then came our young man, our 'Trail Finder,' said he'd hunt the hiding deer-meat, find the tracks of Shakai-katal." (Navaho for *Deer*.)

Third Medicine Man: "After him, there came our archer, 'He Shoots True.' These two together saved our babies, saved our women, saved our pueblo. Let us call them and do honor. Ya-hooooooo!"

(The Medicine Men retire and form a shallow half-circle across back of stage, arms crossed.)

Music: THLAH HEWE.

Song No. 14

Thlah Hewe—Blue Corn Dance (Zuni)

Hi..... ah hai e..... lu.. Shi..... e - e e..... lu

Hi.. e... e..... lu.... Shi.. e.. e..... lu

Lo - wi.. yu te.. a pa.. Ma..... te - o - na ke - si

Lo - wi.. yu te.. a - pa A - wi.. ya - ha - ne Li.....

i - hi - tla... A - hi.. yi... hai E... he.. lu.... wi

ya I yu.. hi yi a ha Hi........... ya ha he

yow.. he yu he yu he yu he yu he yu.....

Natalie Curtis—Indians' Book, p. 442.

To a roll of the tombé, enter, running, from opposite back corners, two archers, in breech clouts and headbands, each carrying a bow and arrow in one hand. They run across the back behind the Chief, passing each other at back center; at each far corner, turn, and run so as to stand either side of the Chief who is at back center. They bow to him, extending both arms backward and downward.

The Chief signs them to proceed. They acknowledge his order with upstage hand raised shoulder high.

They transfer the bows and arrows, so bow is in left hand, arrow in right.

(a) Facing the fire, each step-closes to front, and circles self, holding up bow (1 step-close to each measure)   8 meas.

(b) With toe-flat step, they cross each other in front of fire, to opposite corners, circle selves, bow down and arrow up
13 meas.

(c) Face back, and cross-hop to back   8 meas.

(d) Quickly face front oblique, and shoot across fire to front
3 meas.

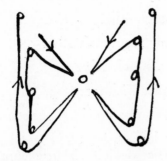

Bow & Arrow (e, etc)

FIG. 36.

(e) Hop-step in to fire   4 meas.

(f) Hop-step away from fire, still facing fire   4 meas.

(g) Hop-step in circle about self   4 meas.

(h) Hop-step half-way down side   4 meas.

(i) Hop-step in circle about self   4 meas.

(j) Hop-step to front   4 meas.

(k) Hop-step in circle about self   4 meas.

(l) Face obliquely toward fire, hop-step in to fire   4 meas.

(m) Hop-step backward out from fire   4 meas.

(n) Hop-step in circle about self   4 meas.

(o) Hop-step to back corner   4 meas.

(p) Hop-step in circle about self   4 meas.

(q) Trot-step to front (2 steps to the measure), and shoot into air, facing obliquely toward each other   8 meas.

83

(*r*) Run across front and up opposite side   8 meas.

(*s*) Kneel, and shoot to back   1 meas.

(*t*) Hop-step backward down to middle of side   4 meas.

(*u*) Kneel, and shoot toward back   1 meas.

(*v*) Hop-step backward down to front corner   4 meas.

(*w*) Kneel and shoot to back   2 meas.

(*x*) Stand, facing front, but head turned toward each other

  4 meas.

(*y*) Scare-step away from each other   4 meas.

(*z*) Trot toward each other   4 meas.

(*a′*) Scare-step away from each other   4 meas.

(*b′*) Trot in to meet each other   4 meas.

(*c′*) Circle each other with trot-step   4 meas.

(*d′*) Pose, facing left, one kneeling, one standing behind   1 meas.

(*e′*) Both shoot to left. Rise, rapid trot around fire, one behind
      the other. The Medicine Man exeunt, walking in time to
      the rhythm, half in either direction, upstage hand raised
      in salute. When they are off, the two archers, with same
      trot-step, exeunt. Use as many measures of music as are
      needed to carry this exit.

Buffalo Dancers.
from Drawing
by Thos. Vigil of Tesuque

FIG. 37.

Rain Dance of Zuni

This dance is always performed at the Pueblo of Zuni on August 19th. Both men and women participate, and all are masked.

The men have long, waved hair; the women wear the hair wrapped at each side with colored worsted around an oblong of cardboard.

The mask of the men is turquoise in color—a straight strip about 6 inches deep, and reaching from ear to ear across the face. At the bottom is a band of painted rectangles, alternately red, blue, and yellow. From this band hangs a horsehair fringe, long enough to hide the throat. There are three white feathers at the top of the mask, one hanging over the face at the middle of the top, and one over each ear. They wear a tuft of macaw feathers on top of the head. (Fig. 38.)

The mask of the women is similar, but white instead of turquoise, and with no colored band above the fringe. There is a short fringe of goat hair around the whole head at the top of the mask. A soft white eagle feather falls over the face, attached above the top fringe.

The men were dressed as follows: The upper body was nude, except for paint, much as in the CORN DANCE, and strings of beads about the neck. A white embroidered apron, and a white knitted sash with ends embroidered in red, black and white. A fox skin hung down the back from the waistline, and evergreens stuck into the belt all around. On the left wrist, a bracelet of silver or leather; the right wrist wrapped in a hank of worsted.

Bare legs, with a tortoise shell rattle tied back of the right knee, and a wide red garter embroidered in white. The left knee tied with black (in some cases dark blue) worsted. Moccasins of bright turquoise blue, about 5 inches high; a turnover of orange at top of either side; trimming of scallops across the front; and a band about 1 1/2 inches wide of quill work tied around the back. (Fig. 36.)

The women were dressed as follows: Absolutely no part of the body or face showed except the feet which were bare. Even the hands were covered by the shawl. A black dress as in the CORN DANCE, with white embroidered underskirt showing about 2 inches. Over the dress, each wore a bright Spanish shawl, some red, some yellow, some flowered, etc. These varied in color and pattern; but over them, each wore another shawl. These over-shawls were square, and of two styles: one all black, the other white, with a border about 10 inches wide top and bottom, of red, striped lengthwise with four hair-lines of white. They wore stockings without feet. They carried a branch of evergreen in either hand, but held much lower than in the CORN DANCE—arms with practically no bend at the elbow.

The woman first in line wore a different mask. Zuni Nick (Utakawi), the ex-governor, who acted as interpreter for us, said this individual was really a man dressed as a woman, and is called a *Habashuka*. This feature of the dance, he said, was taken from a custom at Laguna, though the dance as a whole is Zuni. In ancient times, this part was taken by a real woman, held very sacred by the tribe.

Zuni Mask & Moccasin
FIG. 38.

They worked in two lines, about 4 feet apart, all women in one line, all men in the other.

The main step was alike for both men and women, though a little more vigorously done by the men: Step left foot, step right a little higher, progressing a few inches forward.

They did not work in a circle; but in each of the three figures, progressed along two sides of the quadrangle of the pueblo.

Song No. 15

Zuni Sunset Song

Carlos Troyer—Pub. by Theo. Presser Co., Phila.

Fig. I

(a) Men and women all facing right, to one singing of the song

(b) Continue the step in same rhythm for 8 double steps, but without music

(c) Then the women start the song again, while the men yelp in time (2 yelps to the measure)　　　　　　　　8 meas.

(d) All continue the song to the end　　　　　　　　11 meas.

Fig. II

(a) Men and women facing each other, progression being sidewise　　　　　　　　19 meas.

　(b), (c), and (d) as (b), (c), and (d) of Fig. I　　19 meas.

Fig. III

(a) Men and women all facing left　　　　　　　　19 meas.

　(b), (c), and (d) as (b), (c), and (d) of Fig. I　　19 meas.

There was no drum or tom-tom, but all sang in a loud-soft rhythm. During the singing rests, the time was kept by the clatter of the shells, and the very distinct patter of the moccasined feet.

Zuni Nick says the song varies from year to year, and it is the privilege of all to improvise the new song for each RAIN DANCE.

Dance of the Mudheads at Zuni

The Mudheads represent the primitive people before men became quite men. They are the clowns of the village. During the RAIN DANCE, they had capered about irresponsibly, but now proceeded to have a dance all their own.

FIG. 39.

There were ten of them, costumed as follows: Bodies painted with a light tan clay; each wore a square of black cloth about the neck, and another, a little larger, wrapped around the waistline and hanging to mid-thigh as a breech clout. Most of these were tied about the waist by a rope; one had a rope over the right shoulder, holding up his cloth, more or less inadequately.

The distinctive feature of the Mudhead is the mask. This covers the entire head, front and back, and is made of stockinette, the same tan clay color as their bodies. On the middle of the top is a stuffed bunch about the size of a small orange; one for each ear, one at the middle of the back, and one at the middle of the forehead. For the eyes,

90

there are small holes, with the material of the mask rolled back in a thick circle; similarly a little larger one for the mouth, all three looking exactly like doughnuts, badly baked. A couple had thin horns, also of the stockinette, about three inches long and finger-thick, one over each ear. (Fig. 39.) The leader had a small, soft feather on the left horn. Each carried a rattle; and one Indian in everyday dress, beat the drum.

Standing in a line, one behind the other, the Mudheads shook their rattles in time to the drum, so: 1'-2-3-4-5-rest; 1'-2-3-4-5-rest; 1'-2-3-4-5-rest; 1'-2-3; 1'-2-3.

Now they started to progress forward to this beat, with the single trot-step, varied once in a while with double time for four beats. The rattles sometimes kept the double beat, sometimes beat a steady roll.

At intervals, the whole line faced left—or what would be the center if it were a circle; then back into a line behind each other again.

In about ten minutes, they had completed the circuit of the quadrangle, and the dance ended.

Corn Grinding Song of Zuni

In this, called CORN GRINDING SONG, but more of a *dance* than some others so called, there was a chorus of eight men, among them two flutists and one drummer whose thumper was a hoop of willow.

Enter fourteen women dressed in black with square white shawls, each bearing a large decorated pot on her head. They form an arc at the back, with the chorus in a group at one side, and do not dance.

Enter four girl dancers, each carrying a small brush in her right hand, and a basket tray under her left arm.

A blanket is spread on the ground by the chorus, and a grinding stone laid for each girl. She kneels at her stone, puts her basket alongside, and in rhythm to the music sung by the chorus, sweeps off the stone, places her brush at the right side of her stone; then grinds. At the end of the strain, each sweeps the grindings into her basket.

After a time, the girls rise with brush in right hand, stand in line, then pivot in short steps to right, to left, to right, to left, etc.

Suddenly they pick up the baskets, and exeunt. The pot-bearers and the chorus follow.

The song is simply a part of the everyday life of the Indian maiden—the song she sings when she grinds the corn. Often she invites other maidens to grind corn with her; and they sway to the rhythm of the song. Sometimes, the youths play the flute and drum, or sing to the grinding of the maidens.

The following dance has been developed out of these suggestions:

Song No. 16

Corn Grinding Song (Zuni)

E - lu - ho - ma ya ya.... yal - lan.... ne E - lu - ho - ma ya
ya.... yal - lan... ne yal - lan... ne A - wehlwi - a kwai - i
Im - u - na kwa - gia Lo - nan - esh - to wi - ya - ne He ya.... ha
ya he ya...... Li... wa... ma.... ni - i - yu - te - a - pa
A - wi - ya........ ne Ha - wi - la - na, li......... i... tla.....

Natalie Curtis—The Indians' Book, pp. 433-34.

Corn Grinding Dance of Woodcraft

Before the beginning of the dance, the *metates* (grinding stones) have been put in place in a row, one for each maiden.

(*a*) They walk in, basket under left arm, brush in right hand
12 meas.

(*b*) Each maid, now in front of her *metate*, raises head to the Great Spirit
3 meas.

(*c*) Kneel in place
3 meas.

(*d*) Place brush to right, basket to left
4 meas.

(*e*) Squat back on heels, hands relaxed, look lovingly at *metate*
5 meas.

(*f*) Grind in rhythm
14 meas.
(This completes one rendition of the song)

(*g*) In rhythm, sweep corn into the baskets
8 meas.

(*h*) Stand with basket in both hands
4 meas.

(*i*) Feet together, raise basket to Great Spirit
6 meas.

(*j*) Lower basket toward *Maka Ina* (Mother Earth)
4 meas.

(*k*) Pivot to right, throwing pinch of corn to each of the four winds
5 meas.

(*l*) Encircle *metate* with step No. 21
14 meas.
(This completes the second rendition of song)

(*m*) Face right, and skim (step No. 39) away from *metate* 5 meas.

(*n*) About face, and skim back to *metate*
5 meas.

(*o*) Hold baskets high, all close together
2 meas.

(*p*) Pivot to right
3 meas.

(*q*) Pivot to left
3 meas.

(*r*) String out into one line as in beginning
4 meas.

(*s*) Hold basket high
5 meas.

(*t*) Walk off in rhythm
14 meas.

(This completes the third rendition of the song)

The English translation of the song given by Natalie Curtis is as follows:

> Oh, my lovely mountain,
>   To'yallane!
> Oh, my lovely mountain,
>   To'yallane!
>   To'yallane!
> High up in the sky,
> See the Rain Makers seated,
> Hither come the rain clouds now,
>   He-ya, he-ya, he-ya!
> Behold, yonder
> All will soon be abloom,
> Where the flowers spring,
> Tall shall grow the youthful corn-plants!

Hopi Snake Dance

The SNAKE DANCE is performed by the Hopi Indians on their Reservation in the northeastern part of Arizona. It takes place every year, but at alternate places—one year at Walpi and Mishongnavi, the next at Oraibi, Shungopavi, and Hotevilla. It is the closing public exhibition of a nine-days' secret ceremony in the kivas of the Antelope and Snake Clans.

The exact date is never known until ten days before the dance is to take place. What determines the date, the Whites do not know, though there are various conjectures. Some say it is when the sun casts a shadow from a certain rock in a certain way. However, it is always between the middle and end of August.

The dance is another prayer for rain. The snakes are the emissaries to the Rain Powers, and are held very sacred by the Indians. I shall describe it as we saw it at Mishongnavi on August 21, 1927.

In the center of the plaza was the *kisi*, a sheaf of cottonwood boughs, about ten feet tall and six feet in diameter, hollowed at the front where was hung a square of cloth as a doorway. To one side was a raised pit of stone, covered with a large flat stone lid, where the snakes later retreated.

At about 5 P.M., from the kiva there entered twelve Antelope Priests. They were painted red-brown, with zigzag stripes of white running up and down the upper body. They wore the usual Corn Dance apron, and the sash of the Zuni Rain Dance. From the back of each waistline hung an animal skin—mostly gray foxes, but in other cases, a badger, a cacomistle, a red fox, and a kit fox. On the head was an upright bunch of reddish-brown feathers, which looked like those of a Rhode Island Red rooster. They wore brown skin moccasins, with a self-fringe around the tops. In their hands, they carried each a rattle and a bag of sacred meal.

The step of their entrance was nothing but a vigorous walk in time to their rattles. They marched thus about the whole circle of the plaza four times. Every time they passed in front of the cottonwood bower, each stamped with his right foot on a board sunk into the earth at that point. This board covered a little pit, and had a small hole—the *sipapu* —in the center, representing the entrance to the underworld. The stamping was a message to the nether spirits—to the Great Plumed Waterserpent—that the Snake Dance was about to be performed. Each time they passed the little snake altar, they sprinkled on it sacred meal from their bags.

Finally, they stood in a line in front of the bower, backs to it, and marked time, raising the right foot decidedly higher than the left at each step.

This continued for about two minutes, when there entered from the kiva the Snake Priests, thirteen in number, headed by an albino. Their bodies were painted brown; their faces up to the foreheads, black. The body paint was rubbed off in a six inch oval from either breast and the navel. They wore nothing but a scant breech clout, a skirt of brown leather fringed full length, and brown moccasins. The headdress was of red-brown feathers. In the right hand, each carried a bow, decorated with feathers; also a cottonwood wand about six inches long, tipped with two (in some cases three) eagle feathers. Two young boys (about eight and nine) were of this group.

They entered with a very vigorous march step, oblivious of the crowd, but marching in so wide a circle that the crowd scurried out of their way. They circled the plaza four times, each stamping on the board in front of the booth at each passing.

Finally, they came to position opposite and facing the Antelope Priests, and marked time. The rhythm was kept by the rattles; there was no drum or tom-tom, and, up to this point, no singing.

After a few moments, they began a very soft chanting, inaudible at first, swaying their bodies from side to side, and keeping time with their feather wands. They tapped the wands in air rapidly, twice to the left, twice to the right, etc., nine full times (eighteen double counts). This was done four or five times. Once in a while, they did it three times to each side, then back to the two-rhythm. Evidently they were singing a song to which they were keeping time, though we could not at all times hear their voices. The rhythm seemed to be 1'-2-3-rest; 1'-2-3-rest; that is, loud-soft to left, light-soft to right in the wand movement; but loud-soft to left, light-rest to right in the song rhythm. The music is well given on Victor record No. 20043. I have attempted to notate a portion of this (Song No. 17).

Song No. 17

Snake Dance

Notated by Julia M. Buttree from Victor Record 20043.

After perhaps three minutes of this, they stopped abruptly. One of their number left the ranks, and strolled around in front of the crowd, apparently looking for someone in particular. He finally picked one old Indian, whom he led into the circle of dancers in front of the bower. (Edgar K. Miller, Indian Agent at Keam's Canyon, tells me this is part of an initiation for the old man, who will eventually, after several other trials, be taken into the Snake Order.) It became the duty of the old man to hand out the snakes which were on the ground in the bower, behind the cloth doorway.

The Snake Priests now resolved themselves into groups of three, as follows: No. 2 put his left arm around the neck of No. 1; No. 1 put his right arm around the waist of No. 2; thus they walked very close together. No. 3 walked alone behind this pair. No. 4 as No. 1; No. 5 as No. 2; No. 6 as No. 3, etc.

They began another song, this time louder; and went around the circle once with a march step in which the right foot came up much higher each time than the left. At intervals the right foot was held suspended for two counts of the music.

On the second round, the old initiate handed out a snake, which was taken by No. 1 and held in his mouth about 4 inches back of the head. The tail was draped across the bent left arm. No. 2 kept waving his feather wand in front of the snake's head. No. 4 and No. 5 etc., did the same; while No. 3, No. 6, etc., walked behind each his own pair, until No. 1, No. 4, etc., threw their snakes on the ground. Then No. 3, No. 6, etc., maneuvered the snakes until it was possible to pick them up.

On the next round, a new snake was given to each leader, and the same procedure followed. All told, there were about thirty snakes used

—rattlers, bull snakes, and racers. No. 3, No. 6, etc., finally had their hands full. The snakes hung like strings of boiled spaghetti, soft and squirmy.

Several times it certainly looked as if one of the dancers was struck. Sometimes, the snakes coiled about the throat or the arm of a dancer, so that it was difficult to free it. (Miller says he has seen blood drawn from the face of a dancer by a snake, but these Snake Priests are immune to the poison. And poison there surely is, since nothing is done to the fangs of the snakes to lessen the danger.)

As the Priests began to dance with the snakes, three women came forward on one side, and nine on the other. They wore black shawls like those of the Zuni Rain dancers. At each passing of the Snake Priests, the women sprinkled holy meal on them.

When all the snakes had been used, the dancer of each triad who had been carrying them dropped them to the ground in a circle of meal. Each Snake Priest then grabbed some snakes. Four ran to the east, four to the west, two to the north and two to the south, to return the snakes, now prayer-laden, to the places where they had found them nine days before.

After about an hour, all had returned. They went into the kiva, soon came up clad in nothing but a gee-string, carefully washed their bodies; and then each drank at least a quart of an awful-looking, greenish, brownish, thick liquid provided by two of the women. This emetic may be the reason for their immunity to the poison of the snakes, coupled with the fact that they have been fasting in the kiva for nine days, washing and handling the snakes. Also, no dancer picked up a snake when it was coiled, but used his wand to uncoil it before handling.

I have made no attempt to adapt this dance. If the attitude of a group is serious, I see no reason why it should not be done exactly as described, except for the live snakes. If, however, it is likely to provoke mirth or ridicule, I earnestly urge that it will not be attempted. It is part of the Hopi's religion, and I quote the Woodcraft Law: Reverence the Great Spirit, and respect all worship of Him by others; for none have all the truth, and all who reverently worship have claims on our respect.

The Dancing of the Sioux

At Standing Rock, N. D., among the Sioux, the dancing is entirely different in spirit from that of the Southwest. Among the Pueblos, dancing is distinctly a form of worship or thanksgiving; among the Sioux, it is much more of a social amusement. In the Southwest, it is ceremonial, each dance being done exactly as it has been done for generations, no iota being changed from the stereotyped form prescribed; in the North, in most of the dances, each dancer was a unit unto himself, doing any step he chose at any moment.

At Standing Rock, the best dancing was done in a large wooden building, roughly octagonal in shape, floored with boards. There was above, a central hole, now boarded over, but evidently at one time used as a vent for the smoke of the fire.

At one side, was a huge drum, suspended. The leader wore a head-dress, the other seven dressed in ordinary garb. Some gave quick, soft drum beats; some, terrific loud single beats. Much of the singing was on one note, but with many quavers; and, once in a while, loud ho-ho's. Sometimes, they sang in chorus, sometimes individuals carried it for a line or so. One (always the same, though not the leader) always started the song with a high-pitched keening, and with his finger in his ear, and his eyes screwed up. It was usually soft at first, then a gradual crescendo —sometimes very staccato. Their thumpers were loose at the joint— that is, the stick did not go into the head.

The orchestra started, and the men stood up to dance when the spirit moved them. There was usually most of the group standing in place, marking time with two beats to each foot, almost no lift, chiefly heel work. Then one—and another—and another—would break out into the center of the floor and dance as if he could not help it.

FIGS. 40, 41, 42, 43, 44.

Grass Dance of the Sioux (Pezhi wachipi)

There is always a feast in connection with the GRASS DANCE.

Frances Densmore describes the GRASS DANCE as it used to be done; also records six GRASS DANCE SONGS (*Teton Sioux Music*, pp. 468-477). I reproduce one sung by Two-Shields.

In the GRASS DANCE, the orchestra held up bunches of long grass in one hand, while they thumped with the other.

The dance was a group of solos. Each dancer did any step he wished, changing whenever he liked. Among those I especially noted on the occasion of our feast in July, 1927, were those I have in the Fundamental Steps, as Nos. 6, 7, 8, 9, 10, 11, 12, 13, 14, 15, 16, 17, 18, 22, and 26.

This dance was repeated many times, the dance lasting one minute, the rest period half a minute.

Song No. 18

Song of the Grass Dance (Sioux)

Frances Densmore—Teton Sioux Music, p. 477.

Buffalo Dance of the Sioux (Hatanka)

Both men and women take part in this dance, and all sing. They represent Buffalo. Each carries a bunch of grass in the right hand.

(a) To a soft-loud rhythm, all step-close (No. 1) in one large circle to the left. Both knees are bent a little at each step
12 meas.

(b) Stand still in place, waving the grass   4 meas.

(c) Repeat (a)   12 meas.

(d) Repeat (b)   4 meas.

There are two hunters on the outside of the circle, trotting arm-in-arm throughout.

(e) The circle is now broken. The Buffalo approach each other anywhere, any time, and nudge. One after another, thus killed, sits down.

Sometimes a Buffalo approaches a seated man (or woman), and kicks at his foot. If the sitter wishes, he enters the dance again; if not, he stays dead.

There is a grunting of the Buffalo throughout.

(f) At a sharp beat of the drum, the circle is again formed, all facing outward of the circle, arm-in-arm. Side-step 8 steps as in (a) to the right   8 meas.

(g) 8 steps as above to the left   8 meas.

(h) To right as above   8 meas.

(i) To left as above   8 meas.

(j) Face in, and 8 steps as above, toward center   8 meas.

(k) Still facing in, 8 steps away from center   8 meas.

(l) Jump with both feet at same time to right side   8 meas.

(m) As (l) to left   8 meas.

(n) Standing still in place, wave grass   8 meas.

(o) Face left, hop-step once around circle, and exit   24 meas.

Song No. 19

Dancing Song (Teton Sioux)

Frances Densmore—Teton Sioux Music, p. 147.

Kahomini of the Sioux

There is but one step used throughout the dance: Step left, close right, bending right knee a little and left knee much.

Both men and women dance, in couples. The women invite the men. One man in center of floor calls the figures.

(*a*) Open position, arms about each other's waists, all facing center, side-step as above   3 lines

(*b*) Call from the man in center, and all face partners, holding both hands, step in time backward 2 steps and forward 2 steps
            1 line

(*c*) At call, circle each other once   1 line

(*d*) At call, double line, arms about each other's waists, all going same direction, like the sun   3 lines

(*e*) Step forward left, forward right, back left, back right.   1 line

(*f*) At call, circle once, open position   1 line

Repeat the whole thing.

The dance lasted about 20 minutes, until perspiration streamed.

The Omaha RETURN OF THE RUNNERS carries this dance well (Song No. 20).

FIGS. 45, 46, 47.

Song No. 20

Return of the Runners (Omaha)

Alice C. Fletcher—27th Ann. Rep. Bur. Eth., p. 301.

Song No. 21

Behold the Dawn (Teton Sioux)

Frances Densmore—Holmes Anniversary Volume, Washington, 1916.

Scalp or Wounded Dance of the Sioux

Two war bonnets are hung on a post in the center.
Eight men form in one line, eight women in another, facing the men.

(*a*) All sing (Song No. 21) and keep time in place, raising right
foot higher than the left   21 meas.

(*b*) The women turn to the left, making an inner circle, moving
in the direction of the sun; the men turn to the right, in an
outer circle, moving in the opposite direction. The step is
the same as above, but they progress forward on it now
                                                             19 meas.

A scout is outside the circles, all alone, moving in the same
direction as the men, using the same step but with a sneaky
motion.

(*c*) All stand in place, keeping time, as above   21 meas.

(*d*) Repeat (*b*), but in the opposite direction   19 meas.

(*e*) The head woman puts on one bonnet, the head man puts on
the other, while the music pauses. At this time, a new scout
comes in on horseback (riding a cane)

(*f*) The group have resolved into the two original lines, and again
mark time, and sing; the two scouts parry, etc.   21 meas.

(*g*) One scout falls, the other rides around him in triumph; then
picks him up and takes him off to camp   19 meas.

(*h*) The group forms one circle, makes one round, and exit
                                                             40 meas.

Frances Densmore describes a similar dance of the Utes (*Northern
Ute Music*, pp. 156-57).

The Wind and the Cloud

The cloud is a thin scarf, as large as the dancer can manage.

The dance is accompanied by the tom-tom orchestra (see p. 222), using the TOKALA OLOWAN (Song No. 22).

(a) *Single war drum beat in slow two-part time:*

Hands high, holding cloud overhead, head up, walk to single beat around circle once (1 step to each measure)   10 meas.

(b) *Single beat of war drum; add single beat of tom-toms:*

As above, walk 4   4 meas.

On next walk step, bend knees, and dip cloud to side of forward foot   1 meas.

Walk 4   4 meas.

Dip as above.   1 meas.

Walk 2   2 meas.

Dip as above   1 meas.

(c) *Single beat war drum; tom-toms double beat:*

Run (2 steps to the measure)   5 meas.

(d) *War drum in double time, as well as tom-toms:*

Run 3 steps and dip   2 meas.

Run 5 steps and dip   3 meas.

Run 3 steps and dip   2 meas.

Run 5 steps and dip   3 meas.

(e) *War drum and tom-toms in double time; add single beat with rattles:*

3 short steps forward (left, right, left), and raise right foot forward a little off ground   2 meas.

Repeat   2 meas.

Pirouette, swinging cloud around body   1 meas.

Repeat (e)   5 meas.

1 step forward, and raise other foot forward as above	1 meas.
1 step forward, and raise other foot forward as above	1 meas.
3 steps forward, and raise other foot forward as above	2 meas.
Pirouette, as above	1 meas.
3 steps as above	2 meas.
3 steps as above	2 meas.
Pirouette, as above	1 meas.
3 steps as above	2 meas.
Pirouette as above	1 meas.

(f) *War drum, tom-toms, and rattles double time:*

2 leaps forward, tossing cloud forward	2 meas.
3 hop-steps backward, swinging cloud back	3 meas.
2 leaps as above	2 meas.
3 hop-steps back, as above	3 meas.
2 leaps as above	2 meas.
3 hop-steps back, as above	3 meas.

(g) *War drum, tom-toms, and rattles as above; enter bells on spins:*

8 running steps forward	4 meas.
Rapid spin for the first wind	1 meas.
Repeat for second wind	5 meas.
Repeat for third wind	5 meas.
Repeat for fourth wind	5 meas.
Spin into center of circle	4 meas.

(h) *All instruments get louder and faster:*

Running steps in any direction	10 meas.
Wild spin round and round	4 meas.
Scream and fall	1 meas.

On the fall, all instruments stop abruptly.

Song No. 22

Tokala Olowan—Song of the Fox Society (Dakota)

E ha e... yo e.... yo... he ye ye E ha e... yo

e.... yo.... he ye ye... ye E ha e.... yo e... yo

he ya yo... yo E ha e.... yo e... yo... he ye yo

He ye e ye yo! To - ka - la... ka mi... ye...

ca..... ya... ya na - ke nu... la wa.... on... we....

lo.... We.. ha e..... yo e.... yo.. he ye yo!

Natalie Curtis—The Indians' Book, pp. 73-74.

The Desert Wind

This dance, in distinction to most of the other dances in this volume, is not made up exclusively of Indian steps, as the dancer does not represent an individual, but is the Spirit of the Wind.

Until the storm breaks, the wind can blow from only one direction, so that all the scarf work must keep this in mind.

Unless a very calm day, it will be easier to perform this indoors than out; since, in the open, the real wind might have to be contended with, and be a disturbing factor.

Song No. 23

Gomda Daagya—Wind Song (adapted)

The *music* (Song No. 23) is based on the *Gomda Daagya* from Natalie Curtis' *Indians' Book*, but the theme is adapted to fit the dance routine. The tom-tom orchestra accompanies it throughout, starting with a gentle swishing of the gourd rattles, and gradually adding the small tom-toms, then the larger, deeper ones, and finally the war drum, sticks, bells, etc., etc. (See description of Tom-tom Orchestra, p. 222.)

The *costume* is a white skin dress, fringed all over, cut into ragged points at the bottom. No sleeves, but attached to the arms with elastic bands, a long line of fringe, extending from the fingertips of one hand, across the front, to the fingertips of the other. This fringe on the right hand starts short (perhaps six or eight inches long), and runs longer and longer all the way to the left hand, where it is the full length of the dress. White moccasins on bare feet. Flowing hair.

The *cloud* is a thin, filmy scarf, faintly colored any light shade, or a tie-dyed effect of pastel colors. At the opening of the dance it is lying inconspicuously on the ground at left center.

I (Fig. 48)

(*a*) Enter from right back oblique. Left hand front of face at level of forehead, but not close. Right hand down right back oblique. Keeping body as low as possible, step right foot across in front of left (1-2); step left to left (3); step right foot back across left (4); step left foot to left, and hold, swaying (1-2-3-4)   2 meas.

(*b*) Repeat (*a*), but use pivot instead of hold at the end, landing left foot forward   2 meas.

(*c*) Step right across in front of left (1-2); step left to left (3-4)   1 meas.

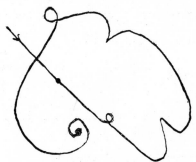

Desert Wind I

FIG. 48.

(*d*) Step right short step backward (1); step left short step backward (2); step right foot short step forward (3); rise on right toe and swing left foot up from ground to left oblique (4)   1 meas.

(*e*) Reverse (*d*), turning to the right   1 meas.

(*f*) Repeat (*d*), turning to back via left (1-2-3-4)   1 meas.

(*g*) 4 little sidewise running steps to left   1 meas.

(*h*) Pirouette   1 meas.

(*i*) Facing back, step left to left (1-2); cross right over left (3-4)   1 meas.

(*j*) Reverse (*d*), turning left   1 meas.

(*k*) Step right front of left (1-2); step left to left (3-4)   1 meas.

(*l*) Pivot   1 meas.

(*m*) Pirouette into center and sink to ground   2 meas.

II (Fig. 49)

(*a*) Slowly rise   4 meas.

(*b*) Take 4 backward steps to left side where cloud lies (4 counts
to each step)   4 meas.

(*c*) Turn to left side toward cloud   2 meas.

(*d*) Stoop toward cloud   2 meas.

(*e*) Pick up cloud, folded in half, and let hang from upraised
hands   4 meas.

(*f*) Softly wave cloud, hands still high   2 meas.

(*g*) Still waving, turn toward center   2 meas.

(*h*) 4 long steps to center (2 counts to each step)   2 meas.

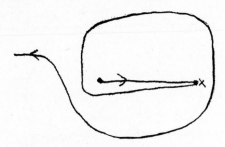

Desert Wind II

FIG. 49.

(*i*) Raise cloud arms' length in front   1 meas.

(*j*) Drop arms in front, left foot taking 1 step back   1 meas.

(*k*) 4 right sidewise steps to back (2 counts to each step) 2 meas.

(*l*) 4 running steps to left side (1 count to each step)   1 meas.

(*m*) 4 running steps to front (1 count to each step)   1 meas.

(*n*) Running steps to right side, where walk into cloud held at
full arms' width   4 meas.

III (Fig. 50)

Hold folded scarf against body, merging wind and cloud
For this figure, use romping step; i.e., step left (1); hop left,
raising right knee, toe pointed down (2); reverse (3-4).

(*a*) Romp back to center   2 meas.

(*b*) Romp forward to right oblique   2 meas.

(c) Romp backward to center   2 meas.

(d) Romp forward to right back oblique   2 meas.

(e) Romp backward to center   2 meas.

(f) Romp forward to left back oblique   2 meas.

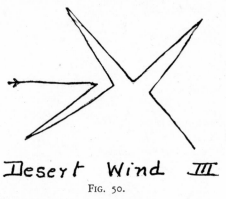

Desert Wind III

FIG. 50.

(g) Romp backward to center   2 meas.

(h) Romp forward to left oblique, swinging cloud out full
length, but holding it near middle of one side, so it hangs
down on either hand   2 meas.

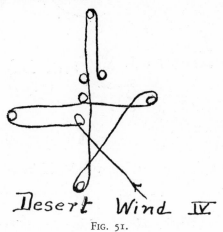

Desert Wind IV

FIG. 51.

IV (Fig. 51)

In this figure, use the following step: Run right (1); run
left (2); leap right forward (3-4).

(a) With this step, cross to center   1 meas.

(b) Pirouette   1 meas.

(c) Go to right   1 meas.

117

(d)	Pirouette	1 meas.
(e)	Go to center	1 meas.
(f)	Pirouette	1 meas.
(g)	Go to left	1 meas.
(h)	Pirouette	1 meas.
(i)	Go to center front	1 meas.
(j)	Pirouette	1 meas.
(k)	Go to center	1 meas.
(l)	Pirouette	1 meas.
(m)	Go to back	1 meas.

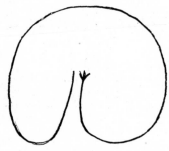

Desert Wind V

FIG. 52.

(n)	Pirouette	1 meas.
(o)	Go to center	1 meas.
(p)	Back pirouette	1 meas.
	All through, wind and unwind self in cloud.	

V (Fig. 52)

Go through entire circle with pantomime of caressing and loving the cloud. Use waltz step with one long hold at end of each measure; i.e., step right (1); step left (&); step left (2); hold, poised on toes (3 & 4)   16 meas.

VI

(a)	In impatience throw cloud to right, full length, holding by one end	1 meas.
(b)	Ditto to left	1 meas.

(*c*) Ditto, throwing up   1 meas.

(*d*) Let crash down in anger   1 meas.

VII

(*a*) With romp step, but with flatter foot as in Sioux hop-step, go round cloud on floor, (2 counts to each step)   4 meas.

(*b*) Snatch up cloud, leap 4 steps to right, (2 counts to each step)   2 meas.

(*c*) Toss it angrily up in air   1 meas.

(*d*) Snatch at end as it falls   1 meas.

(*e*) Leap 4 steps to left (2 counts to each step)   2 meas.

(*f*) Toss it on floor and throw both arms up in vengeance pose, glaring at cloud   2 meas.

VIII

Pick up cloud by one corner. Whirl round and round, dervish turns, whipping cloud like lariat   15 meas.
If using stage with curtain, drop to ground; if not, leap off
                                                                   1 meas.

The Warrior Maiden

The LONE SCOUT, as given by Ernest Thompson Seton in his *Birch Bark Roll of Woodcraft*, has always been popular with the boys. The girls have desired something like it. The following is based on the same dance-thought, but worked around a story justifying performance of a war dance by girls. The general theme is taken directly from Mr. Seton's LONE SCOUT, with just a germ of fact in the story of Pine Leaf, a maiden of the Crow tribe, who has vowed vengeance on the enemy for the death of her twin brother.

The principal song running through this dance is one of the WIND SONGS OF THE KIOWA. Natalie Curtis says (*Indians' Book*, p. 223), Wind Songs (*Gomda-Daagya*) are War Songs "made while the men are on the warpath, and are sung by those at home who think of the distant warriors. . . . As a mother sings a lullaby to the child in her arms, even so she sings to the absent son far away. . . . So might the maiden sing, thinking of her lover. . . . Such songs are called Wind Songs because they are songs of loneliness and longing like the open prairies where there is only the sweep of the wind."

* * *

Pine Leaf arrays herself in the war bonnet of her brother, and starts out with shield and spear. (See Figs. 53 to 56.)

(*a*) She rushes in with a whoop, poses, and takes a few step-hops on her way, when she is met by the Chief of the tribe. He snatches her shield and spear from her, upbraids her for taking up man's work, throws her weapons to the ground, and orders her back to the camp of the women. She slinks off and the Chief retires. (All this is in pantomime, and without music.)

(*b*) When the Chief is safely out of sight she sneaks back, stands for a moment, then sings the Omaha Call, "HEDEWACHI" (Song No. 24) with hands upraised to the Great Spirit at the beginning of the song, but gradually lowered, until she finishes the song on both knees, with head bowed forward on the ground.

Song No. 24

Omaha Call (Hedewachi)

Zha - wa - i - ba.. i..... ba e - he.....

Zha-wa - i - ba i - ba ha......... e - he..............

Alice C. Fletcher—27th Ann. Rep. Bur. Eth., p. 257.

(c) As she slowly raises her head, she espies her weapons. She looks about to make sure she is not seen, cautiously creeps up, and secures her shield and spear. Then, to the music of the *Wind Song*, step-hops around the circle once in triumph (1 step-hop to each measure)   17 meas.

On the last line, step-hop around self, arms back and down, body bent forward at the hips   5 meas.

(d) To MUJE MUKESIN (Song No. 25):

Seek the trail, with toe-flat step (i.e., step forward on right toe (1); drop right foot flat (2); step forward on left toe (1); drop left foot flat (2), etc. (1 toe-flat step to each 2 eighth counts). She uses the various movements of seeking the trail—shading her eyes with her shield, picking up imaginary leaves on the point of her spear and smelling them for traces, stopping to listen for sounds, kneeling with ear to ground, etc., etc.   8 meas.

Song No. 25

Muje Mukesin (Ojibway)

Muj - je muk - e - sin   aw-yaw - yon Muj - je muk - e - sin   aw-yaw - yon

Muj - je muk - e - sin   aw-yaw - yon Muj - je muk - e - sin   aw-yaw-yon

Frederick R. Burton—American Primitive Music, p. 222.

(e) To Tua Wa Washte (Song No. 26):
Still seeking, point step right (1-2); repeat (3-4); walk
right (1); left (2); right (3-4); point left (1-2); repeat
(3-4); walk left (1); right (2); left (3-4), etc.   24 meas.

Song No. 26

Tua Wa Washte (Fox)

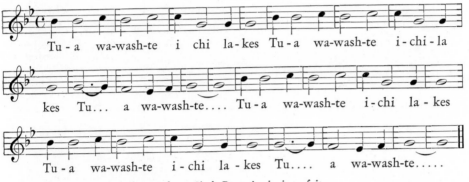

Tu - a wa-wash-te i chi la-kes Tu - a wa-wash-te i - chi - la

kes Tu. . . a wa-wash-te. . . . Tu - a wa-wash-te i - chi la - kes

Tu - a wa-wash-te i - chi la - kes Tu. . . . a wa-wash-te. . . . .

Notated by Julia M. Buttree, from Clark Brown's singing of it.

(f) To Tua Wa Washte (Song No. 26):
Right hand raised, left hand back and down, progressing forward in circle with slow toe-flat step (1 count for toe and 1 for flat)   8 meas.
Reverse hands, and with same step in place, crossing right foot over left, and left over right   4 meas.
Repeat all of (f)   12 meas.

(g) Sharp tom-tom beat, at which she suddenly finds the trail. She drops to one knee, gloating, shakes her fist at the imaginary foe, registering revenge. (No music for this section.)

(h) To the Wind Song (Song No. 24):
She rises, and proceeds to follow the trail, pointing with her forefinger to the ground where it shows. Step forward left (1); step forward right (2); step back left (1); step back right (2)—all short steps and sneaking on toes   22 meas.

(i) To Tua Wa Washte (Song No. 26):
She is frightened by a sound in the forest and starts. Turning to left and crouching with head turned to left, in toward center, both hands palms out to left in front of left cheek, she crosses left foot in front of right (1-2); brings right a little to right without uncrossing (3-4); longer step to right

FIGS. 53, 54, 55, 56.

with left (1-2); right a little to right without uncrossing
(3-4). Repeat, making 4 cross-close steps   4 meas.
Now, hearing a sound in the direction of the center of the
circle, with head to left and hands to right, in toward center,
she reverses the 4 steps   4 meas.
Now, her fear is overcome, and she pivots 4 steps with both
hands raised high overhead, on the pivot progressing to opposite side of the circle   4 meas.
Again becoming frightened, she repeats the whole   12 meas.

(j)   To the WIND SONG (Song No. 24):
She discovers the enemy in the center. She surrounds him
for half the circle, low bent, facing center, step long right
(1-2); close left (1-2); step right (1-2); close left (1-2),
etc.   11 meas.

(k)   To the WIND SONG (very softly) (Song No. 24):
Turn to right, using same step as in (j), but progressing sidewise toward enemy in center. She sneaks up to the enemy
in 4 counts with shield in front of face and spear in right
hand, held back ready to strike. Here the Chief appears in
the entrance, but is unseen by the maiden.

(l)   No music: With one mighty lunge, she strikes and shrieks.
Then she starts to step-hop in triumph, but sees the Chief and
falls back in fear.

(m) The Chief advances, takes the feather from his headband
and puts it in hers.

(n)   To TUA WA WASHTE (very fast) (Song No. 26):
Step-hop in triumph for one round, and exit   24 meas.

Charge of the War Maidens

This is a group dance, corresponding to the solo dance, THE WARRIOR MAIDEN. Tell the same story, except that Pine Leaf's friends come along to help her.

The SONG OF THE FIGHT FOR THE CHARCOAL, AND THE SONG OF THE RED BLANKET carry the dance well.

Use as many girls as desired. Costume—conventional Indian girl's dress, but add war bonnet, shield and spear.

The progression is in a circle unless otherwise stated.

(a) To the music of the CHARCOAL SONG (Song No. 27):
Enter with slow, majestic walk, head very erect; shield on bent left arm in front; right hand holding spear down at side, a little out to back (1 step to each measure)   12 meas.

Song No. 27

Song of the Fight for the Charcoal (Osage)

He-tha wi-tha ha ha He-tha wi-tha ha ha He-tha wi-tha ha ha

He-tha wi-tha ha ha He-tha wi-tha ha ha   He-tha wi-tha ha ha

Alice C. Fletcher—39th Ann. Rep. Bur. Eth., p. 338.

(*b*) Walk in ordinary time, twice as fast as (*a*), (2 steps to each measure), peering from under shield held horizontally at forehead   12 meas.

(*c*) Approaching the enemy. Step-hop, body bent forward (1 step to each measure), both hands held down and rather backward   12 meas.

(*d*) Playing for position. Face center. Cross right foot over left (1&); step left (2&); cross right over left (1&); hop right (2&). Reverse and repeat   12 meas.

(*e*) Change to Red Blanket Song (Song No. 28):
Face right. Walk right (1); walk left (2); stamp right (1&2&); walk left (1); walk right (2); stamp left (1&2&)   4 meas.

Song No. 28

Red Blanket (Ojibway)

Ay-quay-quog-nin-gah de - jah min ne - ne-mo-shayn-nin-gah we - je - ah

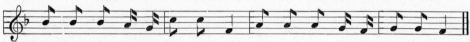

Mis-koo - ah nin-gah-mah - jah - od wah-boy - on nin-gah-mah - je - dun

Frederick R. Burton—American Primitive Music, p. 210.

Step-hop backward 8 times	4 meas.
Walk right (1); walk left (2); stamp right (1&2&); walk left (1); walk right (2); stamp left (1&2&)	4 meas.
Step-hop backward 4 times	2 meas.
Step-hop about self in place, making 1½ turns	2 meas.
Repeat whole in opposite direction	16 meas.

(f) CHARCOAL SONG (Song No. 27):
Face center. Toe-flat step to fire (2 steps to each measure)
2 meas.

Scare step back — 2 meas.

Toe-flat to fire — 2 meas.

Scare step back — 2 meas.

Toe-flat to fire — 2 meas.

Scare step back — 2 meas.

(g) Ready for attack. Step-hop around self — 6 meas.
Pose, right arm up and back, left arm with shield in front, breast-high; weight back on right foot, left toe pointed forward — 2 meas.
Step forward on left foot — 2 meas.
Step forward with right foot, extending spear hand forward and left elbow back a little — 2 meas.

(*h*)   RED BLANKET SONG (Song No. 28):
Sneak step.   Progressing to right, with knees a little bent,
step right to right (1&); step left to right, crossing in front
of right (2&); step right to right (1&); step left to right,
crossing in back of right (2&).   Repeat till song is completed
8 meas.

(*i*)   No music, but tom-tom giving one beat to each step.
Facing half right, step left toward center, close with right,
step left toward center, close with right (8 steps).
Pose with spear up and back, as if taking aim.   Swing spear
in, glaring at point in center of dance space—the enemy;
swing spear out; swing spear in; swing spear out; quickly
pierce center point with spear and shriek, left arm up back,
holding 4 counts.

(*j*)   CHARCOAL SONG (Song 27):
Step-hop off in triumph   12 meas.

Devil Dance of the Apaches

Most primitive peoples have a DEVIL DANCE, in which the Medicine Men dance to exorcise the evil spirits causing disease.

In this case, instead of a drum as accompaniment for the dance, a skin was laid on the ground; five men surrounded it and beat on it with sticks. This is the earliest stage in the development of the drum.

The outstanding feature of this dance, which we saw with slight variation on two occasions, was the huge, weird headdresses worn by the dancers. There were four of these, differing in detail of design, but all about three feet wide, two feet high, elaborately painted and feathered, no doubt symbolically. These four dancers we thought were the Devils, until, on the second performance another dancer entered, with a head-dress much simpler and very different to the others. This was a double cross, standing about one foot into the air. We then decided that he was the Devil, and the other four dancers were Priests or Medicine Men. All five headdresses were mounted on fabric masks which covered the entire head. Even eye- and breath-holes were invisible. This mask was tied about the neck. (See Fig. 57.)

The rest of the costume was a shawl—some of them Scotch plaids—tied about the waistline, and hanging roughly to the knees. The upper body was painted in various designs. There were long streamers, about an inch wide hanging from elbows, wrists and knees. They carried a long (about eighteen inches) double cross in each hand.

The steps throughout were grotesque, low to the ground, very much spread-legged and flat-footed. The attitudes and movements were sharp, ungraceful, sudden. Sometimes one got down on both knees, wide-spread, and rattled his head so that the headdress beat a tattoo upon the ground.

There was no story apparent, but the following could easily be developed:

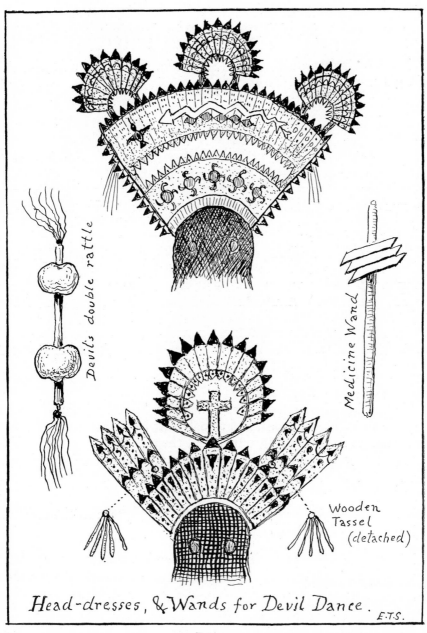

Devil's double rattle

Medicine Wand

Wooden
Tassel
(detached)

Head-dresses, & Wands for Devil Dance.

E·T·S·

FIG. 57.

Devil Dance of Woodcraft

Music: GERONIMO'S SONG (Song No. 29). No drum until so
stated.

Song No. 29

Geronimo's Song

Frances Densmore—Indian School Journal, April, 1906, p. 30.

To a roll of the tombé, enter a Warrior, in full regalia—headdress
of feathers, breach clout, and tomahawk; bells on knees, ankles, etc.
He rushes in to center front, poses, then step-hops (2 steps to the
measure) once across stage, and once around the circle 16 meas.

He continues in full vigor   5 meas.

Enter the Devil, low-crouched, sneaking (2 steps to the measure)
He carries two rattles, as in Fig. 57   5 meas.

He pantomimes glee at finding the Warrior, then tracks the latter
who does not see him at once   6 meas.

The Warrior soon shows that he feels the malign influence. He
tries to continue his animated dance, but gradually limpens. He
tries again, and staggers, then drops down to one knee, rises again,
etc., until, finally he rolls over flat. As the Warrior sinks lower and
lower, the Devil rises taller. (It is impossible to determine the

number of measures of music to this. The dancer must feel and dramatize the story, or not do the dance at all.)

When the Warrior is really down, apparently dead, the Devil approaches, looks him over, then does a dance of triumph about him: Step-hop right, step-hop left, run, run, run almost in place

2 meas.

Step-hop left, step-hop right, run, run, run   2 meas.

Charge forward right, right hand rattle pointed toward dead Warrior   1 meas.

Step back left, step back right, run, run, run   2 meas.

Step back right, pose   1 meas.

Keeping feet still with right foot to the back, twist body toward back foot, and shake rattles (1 shake to each count) holding hands close together and describing circle from right to left   2 meas.

Step-hop left, step-hop right, progressing backward, run, run, run   2 meas.

Charge forward right, pointing as above   1 meas.

Four leaping steps toward Warrior   1 meas.

Pause (1); leap over Warrior (2-3-4)   1 meas.

End with a pose of ghoulish gloating, and a red flash in the fire   1 meas.

(He manages to throw some red flash powder into the fire.)

All through, the accompaniment of the Devil is the sound of his own rattles.

Enter a Medicine Man, slow, dignified, to the accompaniment of the drum. He carries the crossed wand (Fig. 57). No music. The Devil falls back in fear. The Medicine Man approaches steadily. The Devil takes courage, and advances toward the Medicine Man who falls back a few steps. They see-saw back and forth, but the Devil is eventually rather in the ascendancy. The Warrior moves an arm under the power of the Medicine Man, but is downed again by the Devil. The Warrior must play up to these two.

The Medicine Man signals for help.

Music: MIDÉ SONG (Song No. 30):

133

Song No. 30

A Midé Song of the Ojibway

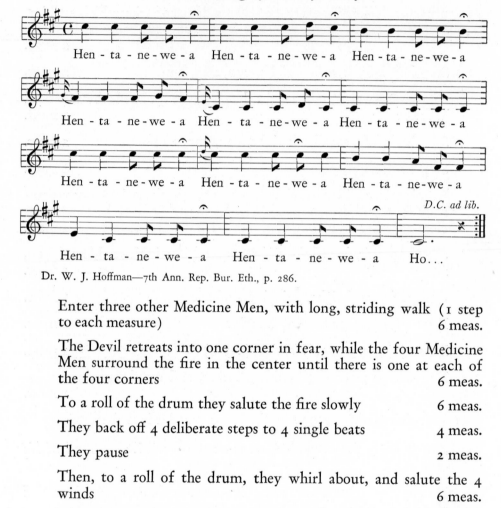

Hen - ta - ne - we - a Hen - ta - ne - we - a Hen - ta - ne - we - a

Hen - ta - ne - we - a Hen - ta - ne - we - a Hen - ta - ne - we - a

Hen - ta - ne - we - a Hen - ta - ne - we - a Hen - ta - ne - we - a

Hen - ta - ne - we - a Hen - ta - ne - we - a Ho...

Dr. W. J. Hoffman—7th Ann. Rep. Bur. Eth., p. 286.

Enter three other Medicine Men, with long, striding walk (1 step to each measure)	6 meas.
The Devil retreats into one corner in fear, while the four Medicine Men surround the fire in the center until there is one at each of the four corners	6 meas.
To a roll of the drum they salute the fire slowly	6 meas.
They back off 4 deliberate steps to 4 single beats	4 meas.
They pause	2 meas.
Then, to a roll of the drum, they whirl about, and salute the 4 winds	6 meas.
They step-hop 8 steps away from the fire (2 steps to each meas.), each in the direction of his own wind	4 meas.
Four step-hops around himself, making 1½ turns	2 meas.
Four toe-flat steps in toward the fire, and 4 about himself	2 meas.
Eight step-hops, backing off	4 meas.
Now all face left, and step-hop once around fire, until the leader reaches the Warrior on the ground	6 meas.

With the sneak step (No. 21), they encircle him, making passes over his body.   To these he responds by gradually rising on one elbow   12 meas.

The Medicine Men, satisfied that he is recovering, step-hop to the other side of the fire.   The Devil has, meanwhile, sneaked up to the patient, and for a moment leaps into the air shaking his rattles violently, at which the Warrior again falls prostrate   6 meas.

The Medicine Men come to the rescue again, driving back the Devil   6 meas.

Finally, the Warrior is evidently recovering, and the Devil is pushed into the background.   As the Warrior finally stands erect, the Devil crumples into a corner.   (This part again must be dramatized by the dancers.)

With the Medicine Men in the attitude of holding back the power of the Devil, the Warrior dances in triumph to the music of GERONIMO'S SONG.

If there is no curtain, so that an exit must be made, the Devil grotesquely jumps up and rushes off; the Medicine Men walk off in dignity, symbols in air, and the Warrior dances off in triumph.

Throughout, the bells mean the Warrior, the rattles the Devil, and the war drum or tombé the Medicine Men.   The force of the instruments must symbolize the dominance of the power behind it. When the Warrior is dead, there is no sound of bells; when the Devil is in the ascendancy, the rattles are strong; before the Medicine Men enter there is no sound of the drum.

The Winnebago War Dance

This dance is performed by two separate groups—the Winnebagos and the Pawnees, their enemies.

To the WARRIOR SONG VI (Song No. 31):

Song No. 31

Warrior Song VI—(Winnebago)

Whi ya he ya whi ya he ya A hi i ya he - e e - e - e

Whi ya he ya whi ya hi ya whi ya he ya whi ya hi ya A ha

i ya he - e - e - e Whi ya he ya whi ya he ya Ha hi o ho

wi ye he - e - e - e - yo Whi ya he ya whi ya he ya Whi ya

he ya whi ya he ya A ha e ya he - e - e - e Whi ya he ya

whi ya he ya Ha hi o ho wi - e He - e - e - e - yo

Natalie Curtis—Indians' Book, p. 286.

(*a*) Enter the Pawnees, with toe-flat step, shading their eyes, and sneaking (1 step to each measure) 9 meas.

(*b*) In a circle, hop-step to right 12 meas.

(*c*) About face, and hop-step to left   10 meas.

>(They keep looking cautiously back to the place of their entrance watching for the Winnebagos.)

(*d*) They decide all is safe and string out into one line, all facing front; back-trot step in place   12 meas.

(*e*) Suddenly, they become alarmed, and all sneak off into one corner at opposite side from entrance, crouching, with bodies turned away from the approaching enemy   10 meas.

To the WARRIOR SONG I (Song No. 32):

Song No. 32

Warrior Song I—(Winnebago)

Shung-ung ke-e   wo-jin wi   ne-e   etc.
Ho..   friend   whip up your   horse   etc.

Natalie Curtis—Indians' Book, p. 275.

(*a*) Enter the Winnebagos, each one astride a cane (his horse), using front-trot step (1 step to each count); close into a circle, looking about for the Pawnees   10 meas.

(*b*) Whirl about, and repeat in opposite direction   15 meas.

(*c*) They line up from front to back of stage, all facing the direc-

tion of the Pawnees, pointing at them menacingly, using step
No. 14   11 meas.

(*d*) The Pawnees rise, face the Winnebagos; and, massed in their
corner, use step No. 28, while the Pawnees continue as
above   15 meas.

To the WARRIOR SONG II (Song No. 33):

Song No. 33

Warrior Song II (Winnebago)

Wa - a we - e la - a ha - a dja - a le - e etc.
See   the   trail they've left   here

He - e he - e   e - e - e - e

Hi - cha ko - lo   Pa - a ni - i na - a wa - a cha - a la - a
Comrades harken   Paw - nee   braves   I   saw   them

Wa - a we - e la - a ga - a ske - e na - a   wa - a we - e
What   a   trail they've left   here   See   the

la - a ha - a dja - a le - e   Wa - a we - e la - a ha - a
trail they've left   here

dja - a le - e

Natalie Curtis—Indians' Book, p. 278.

138

(*a*) The Pawnees, with hop-step, form circle, going to the right. At same time, the Winnebagos form an outer circle, going to left with same step   34 meas.

(*b*) The Pawnees face outward, the Winnebagos inward   2 meas.

(*c*) Each pair (enemies facing) encircle each other with side-close step (1 step-close to each measure)   12 meas.

(*d*) Suddenly the Pawnees dash outward through the line of the Winnebagos, running off in all directions; while the Winnebagos, surprised, stand still, looking after them   6 meas.

(*e*) The Winnebagos hop-step around in triumph, and exeunt

10 meas.

The Story Dance

Chief Buffalo Child Long Lance in his biography, tells of a Blackfoot dance which he calls the I SAW DANCE. In this, each warrior reenacts in a dance before the tribe some glorious event of his past life.

This suggests an interesting competitive dance which will appeal to the imaginations of our groups.

Have all seated in a circle, the drummers in one spot to the side where they are out of the way, but clearly audible, and where they can easily see the feet of the dancers.

The orchestra starts a dance song of any kind, for instance, THE RETURNING HUNTER (Song No. 34). Suddenly, one of the circle stands, marks time in place until all are looking at him. Then he comes forth into the center of the floor, and dances out his story—that is, tells the story in rhythmic pantomime.

Song No. 34

The Returning Hunter (Eskimo)

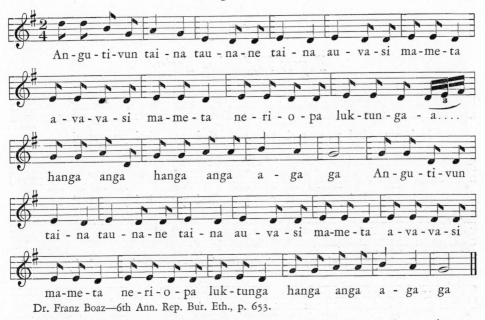

An - gu - ti-vun tai - na tau - na - ne tai - na au - va - si ma - me - ta
a - va - va - si ma - me - ta ne - ri - o - pa luk - tun - ga - a....
hanga anga hanga anga a - ga ga An - gu - ti - vun
tai - na tau - na - ne tai - na au - va - si ma - me - ta a - va - va - si
ma - me - ta ne - ri - o - pa luk - tunga hanga anga a - ga ga

Dr. Franz Boaz—6th Ann. Rep. Bur. Eth., p. 653.

When he finishes, he dances back to his place in the circle, to the applause of the group. Without any hint from the dancer, the group write down what they think the story was.

Another, to whom this performance has suggested new ideas, rises, and marks time in place as did the other dancer. When attention is all on him, he advances and dances his narrative.

These need not be war dances, as probably they were in Long Lance's day. They may be any kind of story the dancer wishes to tell. For example: "I went out in the woods. I saw a snake. I ran home." Or, "I went out in the woods. I saw a woodpecker. He was tapping on a tree. He had a beautiful red head. I watched him until he flew away."

If the dancer wishes to dance in a rhythm other than that being played by the orchestra, he does so, and the leader of the chorus falls in with him. The leader must be one who can follow the changes of rhythm which the dancer may introduce; a clever leader can do much to further the success of the dances.

The winner is the one whose dance made the greatest number of right guesses possible.

Dance of the Moons

The PEYOTE DRINKING SONG might be used for this. (Song No. 35.)

Song No. 35
Peyote Drinking Song

Hai yu hai yu wat-si na yu Hai yu hai yu wat-si na yu

Hai yu hai yu wat-si na yu Hai yu hai yu wat-si na yu

Hai ni yu Hai yu hai yu wat-si na yu Hai yu hai yu wat-si

na yu Hai yu hai yu wat-si na yu Hai yu hai yu wat-si

na yu Hai ni yu Hai yu hai yu wat-si na yu Hai yu

hai yu wat-si na yu Hai yu Hai yu wat-si na yu Hai ni yu

Julia M. Buttree—Recorded from Pedro Nieto, Santa Fe, N. M., Aug. 7, 1927.

This is a dance for the night of the full moon.

Choose a high spot in the open where a clear view of the moon is possible.

The dance, as here given, is planned for sixteen maidens, but can easily be adapted to other numbers, or to include boys.

Number the dancers in two groups, each from 1 to 8.

(1) Run around circle once, and finish, facing each other in two
vertical lines, No. 1's at the front. (Fig. 58) 9 meas.

(2) With toe-flat step, each progresses forward, passing between
the two who come from the other side, right shoulders passing. (Fig. 59) 9 meas.

Moon Dance (1)

FIG. 58.

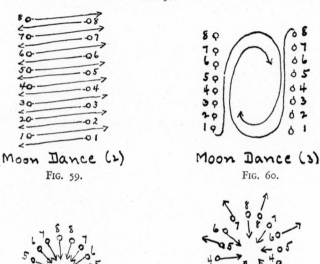

Moon Dance (2)

FIG. 59.

Moon Dance (3)

FIG. 60.

Moon Dance (4)

FIG. 61.

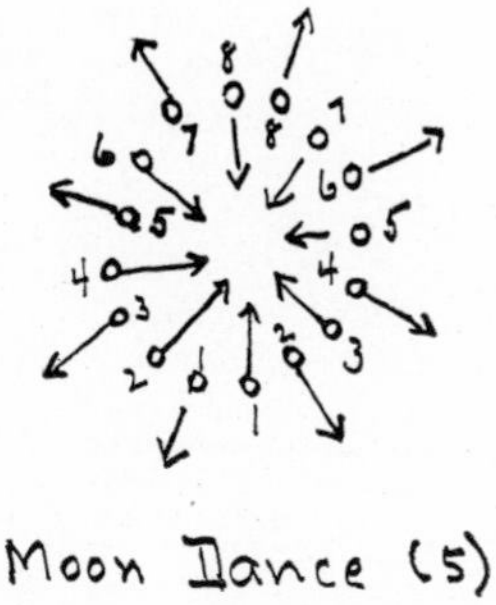

Moon Dance (5)

FIG. 62.

(3) One line faces back, the other front. With hop-step, bending
body forward and backward at hips, No. 1 leads one line, No.
8 the other, in direction of Fig. 60, until one large circle is
again formed, all facing center 7 meas.

(4) Join hands. With rock-and-hop step, progress toward center;
on the second hop, turning about, and repeating until back in
large circle. (Fig. 61) 8 meas.

143

(5) Every other one faces outward   1 meas.

Now each progresses forward with cross-hop step—3 counts forward, 3 counts about self, 3 counts backward, 3 counts about self   8 meas.

All face left.   (Fig. 62)   1 meas.

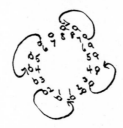

Moon Dance (6)

FIG. 63.

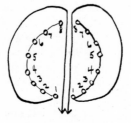

Moon Dance (7)

FIG. 64.

(6) With toe-heel-hop, move about in 4 small circles to the left. (Fig. 63)   7 meas.

(7) When back in places, follow both No. 1's, around and down center, meeting corresponding number of other side, and exit with hop-step in pairs (Fig. 64) to as much music as is needed.

The Sun Dance

The SUN DANCE was common among all the Plains tribes. The picture called up in most White minds at the mention of a SUN DANCE is a gory group of men tied to a pole by thongs which eventually pull free through the flesh. The torture inflicted in this dance was very real in some cases, but it was not nearly so general as is commonly thought.

In some tribes torture was not employed at all; and even in those that included it, it was a very minor and non-essential part of the whole ceremony.

SUN DANCE is the name given to it by the Whites. Among the Arapahoes it was called the OFFERING; among the Cheyenne, the NEW-LIFE LODGE.

George A. Dorsey, who made an elaborate study of the SUN DANCE, says: "According to the interpretation of the priest, the name means not only the lodge of new life, or lodge of new birth, but it is also the new life itself. The performance of the ceremony is supposed to re-create, to re-form, to re-animate the earth, vegetation, animal life, etc.; hence it would not be inappropriate to speak of the Sun Dance as the ceremony of rebirth or of the renaissance." (*The Cheyenne*, "The Sun Dance," p. 57.)

Out of various elements of the dance, as performed by different tribes, I have assembled the following:

The Sun Dance of the Woodcraft Indians

The Sun Dance pole, representing the sun, has been placed at the outer edge of the circle, opposite the Council Rock. In the center is a hung drum (see Fig. 77), around which the orchestra are seated.

Song No. 36

Sun Dance Song (Cheyenne)

E ya ha we.. ye he ye ye he ye.. ho we.. ye

whi ye ye E ya ha we.. ye he ye ye He ye.. ho

we.. ye hai i yi hi ha Hi.. yi ha i....... ya

ha ya ya Ha ai ya ha ai yo yu ai ye ye Ha ai yu ho

ho o yu Ho ai ho ho ho - o yu He ye he a ya

Natalie Curtis—Indians' Book, pp. 166-67.

Enter four Old Men symbolizing the World-quarters. Each wears a headdress surmounted by an animal totem, significant of the quarter he embodies—a White Rabbit for the North, a Red Wolf for the East, a Badger for the South, and a Gray Bear for the West.

They make one round of the circle, with a simple, slow walk, arms folded (14 meas.). They stand each in his place as indicated by the X in Fig. 65 (1 meas.). They raise both hands in silence to the Great Spirit (7 meas.); then sit in place (2 meas.).

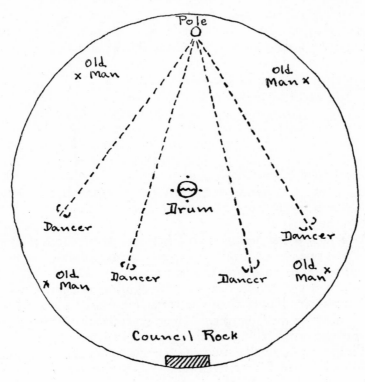

Fig. 65 - Plan of the Sun Dance
of the
Woodcraft Indians

Fig. 66 - Prayer Plume

FIGS. 65, 66.

A chorus of eagle whistles is heard off-stage. Enter four Sun Dancers, in breech clouts, each wearing a sun wreath as in Fig. 90, and in his mouth a bone whistle hung by a cord around his neck. The whistles symbolize the breath or life of man.

Each dancer carries at waist level in front of him, a buffalo skull (Fig. 90). Looking straight ahead they march briskly around the circle, to a single, measured beat of the drum. There is no music to this, but a steady blowing of the whistles.

When they reach their appointed places, as indicated by the horns in Fig. 65, they stand still, and stop blowing. They let the whistles fall from their mouths. After a pause of a moment they suddenly, in unison, raise the skulls at arms' length, and sing the SUN DANCE SONG (Song No. 36). 24 meas.

Then, to the same music, but in strong dance rhythm, they begin to dance in four straight lines toward the pole and back. From now on, they do not try to keep together. The object is for each to hang his skull on the sun-pole.

After a few moments one of them staggers, but recovers. He is to be the first one to succumb. Now and again one shows signs of weakening, but struggles back into the dance until he actually falls prone to the ground, then crawls off, dragging his skull after him.

One remains longer than the rest. He must be a good actor as well as a vigorous-bodied dancer. After several vain attempts to hang his skull on the pole, falling to the ground in weakness, recovering, again dropping, etc., he finally succeeds. For a moment, he hangs limp to the pole himself; then, his strength renewed, he dances off in good form.

Green Corn Dance of Santo Domingo

During the year a number of Indian couples have been married according to their own customs; but on August fourth of each year, these marriages must be sanctified in the Catholic Church. The ceremony is simple and sweet, and acceded to by the Indians without enthusiasm either way. They know they have been married anyway, but since the Whites so desire it, they will humor them by going through the form of marriage as moderns see it.

Dr. Edgar L. Hewett says: "It has nothing whatever to do with the conception of the universe which the Redman entertains and is convinced of. It is easy for him to tolerate the Christian intrusion, since it represents for him one more belief in the unquestionable goodness in things around him. It is otherwise as foreign to them essentially as all white attempts upon the Red soul inevitably must be." (*Art and Archæology*, March, 1922, pp. 114-115.)

On this day in 1927, we arrived at the pueblo just as the Recessional was coming from the church. A kettle drum led the crowd, beating loud-soft-soft-loud-loud-soft—really a rapid 6/8 time. This was followed by the Catholic Priest, then an Indian carrying the Cross. A group of about ten young Indian boys came next, each carrying a tall white candle; then four boys each holding one corner of a canopy under which was the image of Santo Domingo, borne by four men. The saint had been adorned for the occasion by a new colored silk hanky about his neck.* Behind the image of Santo Domingo came the newly-weds, couple by couple; after them, the rabble, all chanting softly.

The Recessional paraded through all the streets of the village, ending at a bower built as the repository of the Saint for the day. This was at one end of the plaza where the CORN DANCE was to go on all afternoon. An old Indian bearing a gun stayed on guard at the booth all day to keep off the evil spirits.

* * *

An Indian, in accordance with the prevailing clan system, is born either a Summer (*Calabash*) Indian, or a Winter (*Turquoise*) Indian, though this has no relation to the season of his birth; and so he must always remain. There are, therefore, in Santo Domingo, two kivas (or

---

* The silk hankies of most brilliant color in the Southwestern small-town trading stores are those favored by the cowboys—in purple, green and pink combinations, and across the center of which are the words: "Let 'er buck." Such was the neckerchief of Santo Domingo, reverently placed there by these simple-hearted believers.

estufas, as they call them here)—one for the Summer people and one for the Winter.

* * *

Everyone in the pueblo is supposed to participate in the ceremony of the CORN DANCE. It is not only an invocation, but a thanksgiving.

At 11:30 A.M., there issued from each kiva a group of Koshare, eleven in one group, and ten in the other. The Koshare are a secret order of which the Whites know very little, except that the order is dying out. There are about twenty-five members in this pueblo, but in some it is reduced to two. We do not know what the qualifications are, but realize that these individuals are held in high esteem by the other inhabitants. They represent the ancestral spirits of the people and are supposed to be invisible to the rest of the pueblo.

FIG. 67.

Before their appearance for this dance, they have been purified in the kiva by the Rainbow Woman. This woman is held very sacred in the tribe, but no White knows who she is.

According to the ancient legend, when the Indians first came into the world, they were much beset by hardships. They were finally reduced to such straits that they lost courage and became disheartened. This made matters worse until the gods, in order to make them forget their troubles, painted one of their number white, and decorated him most fantastically. This Koshare, Dancing Man, or "Delight Maker," as Bandelier calls him, came among the people and capered and danced until his antics made them laugh. Thus encouraged, they again took up their burden and carried on to triumph.

* * *

For the ceremony of the CORN DANCE the Koshare were dressed as follows (see Fig. 67): Their bodies were painted mostly white with round spots of black all over. Several had one whole leg blue. One group wore branches of evergreens across the breast and back from shoulder to hip. The other group were entirely nude above the waist, except for paint.

Each wore a ragged square of black cloth about the neck, hanging some eight inches down chest and back. A strip of black rag was knotted about each wrist and below each knee.

A belt of cloth was strung with rattles. The breech clout was a long strip of black cloth, passing between the legs, slung over the belt and hanging in apron effect front and back.

Branches of spruce were tied about the ankles. Some wore moccasins, others were barefoot; rattles and anklets of beef toes and turtle shells completed the costume.

Their hair was pulled up tight from the head all around, and painted white like their bodies, then rolled up in a knot at the top; for head-dress, a bunch of dried corn-husks, points up.

Each carried a gourd rattle in the right hand.

They marched through all the streets of the pueblo, singing, and vigorously shaking their rattles, moving both hands in unison to each two counts. The song is strongly accented on the first count of each four, thus:

> Huh' huh huh huh
> Huh' huh huh huh;

and is sung in a very fast tempo; but has very little melody, and no words —merely vocables in strong rhythmic chant.

* * *

At 1 P.M., led by the standard (called *tiponi*), there entered the plaza forty-eight couples—man, woman, man, woman—the women a little diagonally behind the men. The men used the back-trot step, the women walked in the same rhythm, but without the lift.

The women wore black cloth dresses reaching to their calves. The right arm was covered with a short sleeve, the left arm and shoulder bare. A red underskirt showed about one inch under the black dress; and under that, a white embroidered petticoat hung about two inches longer. A knitted belt of red worsted, striped in thin white and black, was tied about the waistline, the two ends hanging down the right side. The feet were bare.

In each hand they carried a bunch of evergreen which they moved alternately in time to the music. The arms were held close to the body from shoulder to elbow. The hands were turned rather out to the sides; the movement was entirely from the wrist.

All wore their beautiful glossy hair hanging; in most cases it was long enough to reach the thighs.

The headdress (called *tablita*) was of thin wood, turquoise color, cut in three terraces at the top edge. The center one was turquoise like the main part, the two side ones yellow on the front, red on the back. Near the center were various geometric figures cut out of the wood. Two soft white feathers hung from each outer point at the top, and two half-way down each side. These *tablitas* were tied under the chin to keep them in place.

Every detail of the costume has a symbolic meaning.

*   *   *

The costume of the men was as follows: The upper body was nude except for a strip of conue shells from right shoulder to left hip, and strings of beads about the neck. All had one large brilliant shell at the front of the throat.

On each arm, just above the elbow, they wore a band of turquoise buckskin, about four inches wide, some straight-edged, some terraced. These held branches of evergreen close to the outside of the arm. The bands closed on the inside of the arm to within about two inches, then laced.

Each wore a short white apron of native weave, embroidered in colored wools—green, red, and black—with symbols of clouds, earth and rain. Hanging down the back from the waistline was a gray fox skin, the brush almost reaching the ground. A string of bells encircled the waist.

Under the knees each had tied a hank of green and black worsted. Some had bells on one leg. The right forearm and foreleg were painted in a symbolic pattern in white zigzag lines—probably lightning.

Each carried a rattle in the right hand and a branch of spruce in the left. Their hands worked simultaneously, not alternately like the women's.

They wore the hair in a thick bang to the brows, bobbed square at the sides just below the ear; then most were long at the back, though a few progressives were bobbed all around.

The headdress was a tuft of short, green, soft macaw feathers.

All wore branches of spruce tied about the ankles, and moccasins with a broad band of skunk skin, black at the top, with a fringe of white at the bottom.

*   *   *

On the one side was massed the chorus—"solid like a cluster of bees" —eighty-seven in one group, forty-nine in the other; mostly old or elderly. There was a drummer for each group who stood at the front and beat the tombé vigorously. There was also for each group a leader who called out what was probably the figures of the dance, or maybe the phases of the song. All were clad in long, loose pants, and loose shirts

152

of brilliant colors, bright belts, and head-hankies about the forehead. They wore the hair in a hanging knot at the back about four inches long, tied with a hank of colored worsted. All used their hands in uniform gestures.

The song consisted of about ten phrases, repeated over and over again all day. It started with an explosion, the first line high in the scale; then diminishing in force and dropping into the lower notes of the scale, as do the climaxes of most Indian songs. There were many quarter-tones or quavers, almost impossible to imitate; but no part singing. The drum beat was not accented in any definite rhythm—just a fast, steady, vigorous thumping.

*   *   *

There was a *tiponi* or standard for each kiva. During the rest period, it stood on the roof of its kiva as a sign that the dancers were within.

*   *   *

Each round of dancing lasted forty minutes; toward the close of which period the dancing group would gradually progress in the direction of its kiva, while the other group, which had been resting for the time, came in to the same rhythm. In this way, there was never a break in the song.

*   *   *

The Koshare are remarkably graceful dancers. They did not follow the figures of the group, but wound in and out among them, "like queer spotted dogs," no two working together. There seemed to be in the movements of their flexible hands certain stereotyped gestures, "calling something down from . . . sky, calling something up from . . . earth." (D. H. Lawrence, *Theatre Arts Monthly*, July, 1924, p. 456.) But these gestures have become so ritualized that it is almost impossible to identify them.

Often, one would dance about, looking under one hand which shaded his eyes, as if seeking something. There were many rapid twists of direction.

These Koshare were invisible to the dancers, but toward the end of the day one would occasionally speak to a dancer as he passed, evidently keeping up the spirits.

Within the large group of dancers the men did the sharp back-trot step, lifting the foot high behind at each snap of the knee. It was extremely strenuous, though monotonous. "The ripple of bells on knee-garters, the seedlike shudder of gourd rattles, great necklaces of shell cores springing on their naked breasts, neck shells flapping up and down, kept time to the hopping leap of the dance, the strong lifting of the knees, the downward plunge of the feet in buckskin boots, coming down with a lovely, heavy, soft precision, first one, then the other, dropping always plumb to earth."

The dance of the women was, on the face of it, monotonous. They did practically nothing but the shuffle step, the only motion a short step to the side, scarcely moving, yet edging rhythmically along with flat feet "that seemed to cleave to earth softly and softly lift away. . . . They keep the body quite erect, alternately advancing either shoulder slightly, which gives them a peculiar swaying or rocking motion, like the waving of a wind-rocked stalk of corn."

There is a peculiar vibration of the whole body. Every cord in the foot, running up from the toes, moves in time to the music. "Noted closely, it will be seen that the whole flesh is quivering with the rhythm of the drum."

Sometimes there was a very short progression backwards, so that the track of the big toe was like a ripple of the sand. (Fig. 74.)

At intervals during the dance, the upper end of the standard was lowered and waved over the group. This is the blessing, and every individual passes under it at some time during the day.

The main figures of the dance were as follows (see Figs. 68 to 73): *

Fig. I. The women close, but diagonally behind the men in 2 rows—really making 4 lines. All face right and progress forward in that direction, using the back-trot step (2 steps to each measure, except in the 9th, 10th, and 31st measures, where the time changes to three-part rhythm). In these 3 measures trot on 1st count, and hold foot up behind for other 2 counts; then continue as before   45 meas.

Fig. II. The couples facing each other in two long lines trot-step in place. Then they weave in and out with opposite couples, the woman always remaining behind the man, stepping exactly as in I   45 meas.

Fig. III. In one long line, following the leader around, and re-forming in one long line, stepping as in I   45 meas.

Fig. IV. (a) Each group of 6 couples circling, then resolving into (b) two perpendicular lines for each circle   45 meas.

Fig. V. As in IV (a), then resolving into two horizontal lines for each circle   45 meas.

* * *

At 6:15 P.M., instead of the dancing group preparing to rest, the two groups, Summer and Winter, danced toward each other. They did not sing or dance the same part at the same time, but more in the manner of a round. They did not mingle, but the "two singings, like two great winds, surged one past the other" (Lawrence), then back again.

After about twenty minutes of this, one group, to the sound of a

* The white circles represent the men, the black circles the women. The tiny line out of each circle is the direction of the face.

rifle and the kettle drum, marched in single file into the bower where the image of Santo Domingo had watched the dance all day; paid their respects, and passed on into its kiva.

The other group continued to dance about forty minutes longer, then did likewise. Santo Domingo was then reverently raised and carried

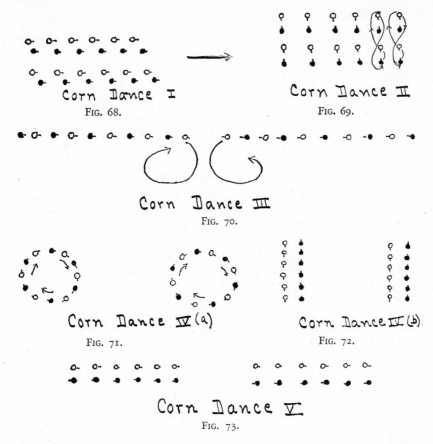

Corn Dance I
FIG. 68.

Corn Dance II
FIG. 69.

Corn Dance III
FIG. 70.

Corn Dance IV (a)
FIG. 71.

Corn Dance IV (b)
FIG. 72.

Corn Dance V
FIG. 73.

back into the church in the same manner in which he had been brought out in the morning.

These dancers had fasted all the day of the dance, perhaps longer (some say three days). The women now carried into the kivas huge baskets of bread, bowls of soup, etc. They break their fast in a feast.

* * *

Song No. 37

Shoko Otïïkwe—Corn Dance Song (Zuni)

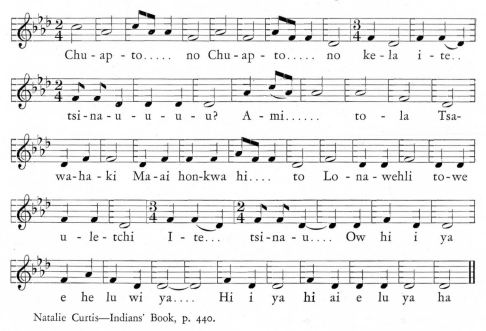

Chu - ap - to..... no Chu - ap - to..... no ke - la i - te..

tsi - na - u - u - u - u? A - mi...... to - la Tsa-

wa - ha - ki Ma - ai hon - kwa hi.... to Lo - na - wehli to - we

u - le - tchi I - te... tsi - na - u.... Ow hi i ya

e he lu wi ya.... Hi i ya hi ai e lu ya ha

Natalie Curtis—Indians' Book, p. 440.

So much for bare, observational details, easy enough to note down early in the day. But, by late afternoon the atmosphere that pervaded the place was of another world.

All day without a break of rhythm, the alternation of the Summer and Winter dancers had continued in a prayer of intense, sustained fervor. All day the vigor of the dance had gradually increased, until by sunset there was an accumulation of force and uplift that penetrated the spectators as well as bound the dancers. There was a hypnotic spell over all. "The blended effect . . . was an organic pæan in praise of life. All the dancers were united in a flame of massed movement which caught the beholders in a similar flame of passionate life."

It was no longer possible to follow the steps or see individuals. It had become a rhythm of mad color—the blue of the *tablitas* almost still, the other colors wildly but rhythmically bobbing. It had lost its character as a dance—it was pure emotion.

The dust, the houses, the ground, the air, vibrated with the prayer of the dancers. The pattern of their feet on the floor of the plaza was like watered silk. The music of the dance had passed into the earth, and was made visible.

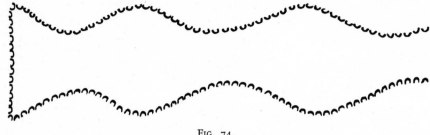

FIG. 74.

The rhythm of their prayer, "a rhythm more deep than that of any music," had rocked the air and the clouds. It was something more powerful than prayer—it brought to pass that which it desired to accomplish.

For, swift with the cessation of the dance, came the rain.

PART TWO
CEREMONIES

Introducing the Child to the Universe

The Omaha have a ceremony which is paralleled in some form among most Indian tribes. It is that of introducing the newborn child to the Cosmos.

Alice C. Fletcher has described this as follows:

"This ritual was a supplication to the powers of the heavens, the air, and the earth for the safety of the child from birth to old age. In it, the life of the infant is pictured as about to travel a rugged road stretching over four hills, marking the stages of infancy, youth, manhood, and old age.

"The ceremony which finds oral expression in this ritual voices in no uncertain manner the Omaha belief in man's relation to the visible powers of the heavens and in the interdependence of all forms of life. . . . It expresses the emotions of the human soul, touched with the love of offspring, alone with the might of nature, and companioned only by the living creatures whose friendliness must be sought if life is to be secure on its journey." (*27th Ann. Rep., Bur. Eth.,* p. 115.)

This ceremony takes place when the child is eight days old. At the appointed time, the priest is sent for. When he arrives, he takes his place at the door of the tent in which the child lies, and raising his right hand to the sky, palm outward, he intones the following in a loud, ringing voice:

Priest

"Ho! Ye Sun, Moon, Stars, all ye that move in the heavens,
    I bid you hear me!"

Group

"Into your midst has come a new life.
    Consent ye, I implore!
Make its path smooth, that it may reach the brow of the first hill!"

Priest

"Ho! Ye Winds, Clouds, Rain, Mist, all ye that move in the air,
    I bid you hear me!"

Group

"Into your midst has come a new life.
    Consent ye, I implore!
Make its path smooth, that it may reach the brow of the second hill!"

"Ho! Ye Hills, Valleys, Rivers, Lakes, Trees, Grasses, all ye of the earth
I bid you hear me!"

Group

"Into your midst has come a new life.
    Consent ye, I implore!
Make its path smooth, that it may reach the brow of the third hill!"

Priest

"Ho! Ye Birds, great and small, that fly in the air,
Ho! Ye Animals, great and small, that dwell in the forest,
Ho! Ye Insects that creep among the grasses and burrow in the ground,
    I bid you hear me!"

Group

"Into your midst has come a new life.
    Consent ye, I implore!
Make its path smooth, that it may reach the brow of the fourth hill!"

Priest

"Ho! All ye of the heavens, all ye of the air, all ye of the earth:
    I bid you all to hear me!"

Group

"Into your midst has come a new life.
    Consent ye, consent ye all, I implore!
Make its path smooth—then shall it travel beyond the four hills!"

When moccasins were made for a little baby, a small hole was cut in the sole of one, so that "if a messenger from the spirit world should come and say to the child, 'I have come for you,' the child could answer, 'I cannot go on a journey; my moccasins are worn out.' The new (whole) moccasins put on the child at the close of the ceremony of introducing it into the tribe (when it is about four years old), constitute an assurance that it is prepared for the journey of life, and that the journey will be a long one."

Bringing in the Fire

In our Woodcraft councils, we aim to light the Sacred Fire with the rubbing sticks in the ancient way of the woods. But occasionally this is impracticable for one reason or another, and it is necessary to do it otherwise. Various methods are possible; the only one impossible is to use the matches of the White man.

The following is a form we have used with success:

The Chief sends a messenger for the Fire Maiden. The messenger returns, salutes at the entrance, and pantomimes the approach of the Fire Maiden.

A chanting is heard from a distance. It draws nigh, and the Fire Maiden enters, holding a bowl of fire high above her head in both hands. She stands for a moment in this pose at the entrance. When given a sign of permission by the Chief, she walks across to center, turns downstage and stands in same pose behind the altar in which the Fire is prepared.

The four Law Reciters follow in a straight line on her entrance, hands relaxed at their sides, heads bowed. They form a straight line across the back behind the Fire Maiden.

The Chief advances to his side of the altar and stands. The Fire Maiden drops to one knee, and the Chief takes the Fire from her. He empties this on to the prepared altar wood. At the first blaze, the Fire Maiden rises, and the four behind raise their heads and hands.

The Fire Maiden takes four torches from her girdle, holds them in both hands, over the now blazing Fire, and says: "As the Great Central Fire of all reaches out to the four corners of the earth, and kindles blazing lights, so at our sacred symbol Fire light we our lamps—one each for Beauty (the first Law Reciter steps forward, receives her torch and takes her position at her lamp); Truth (the second Law Reciter as above); Fortitude (ditto for the third); and Love (ditto for the fourth). And while these lights are blazing bright, we know that we shall grow." (See *Birch Bark Rolls*, early editions.)

The Law Reciters get down on both knees, and squat back.

The Fire Maiden continues: "Four candles are there on the shrine of this, our symbol Fire. And from them reach twelve rays—twelve golden strands of this, the Law we hold."

The Fire Maiden retires a little. The first Law Reciter gets up on to one knee, lights her torch at the Central Fire, and says: "From the

Great Central Fire, I light this, the Lamp of Beauty." Then she recites her three laws, and sinks back on to her two knees.

Ditto for the other three Law Reciters.

When the last one is finished, all rise, and salute the Chief. He returns the salute and hands back the bowl to the Fire Maiden, who briskly leads off.

The Peace Pipe Ceremony

In the early editions of the *Birch Bark Roll of Woodcraft*, Ernest Thompson Seton has given a Peace Pipe Ceremony, to which he refers in his chapter on Peace Pipes (p. 257).

Using this as the main feature, I enlarged the ceremony for the 1925 edition, essentially as follows:

The Chief rises from the Council Rock, and calls: "Ho, Channung-pa Yuha, O-hay!" (Oh, Pipe-bearer, bring the Pipe!)

Singing of the Zuni Sunrise Call (as below) is heard in the distance.

Then, enter the Herald, staff in hand. He faces the Chief, at the opposite side of the Fire, and sings the Sunrise Call again, but omitting every other line which is softly sung off-stage as an echo.

Song No. 38

Zuni Sunrise Call

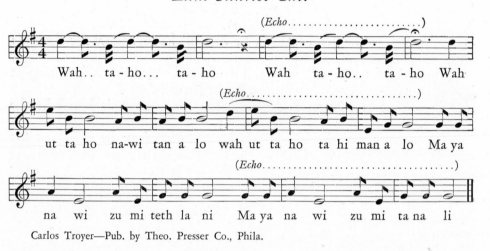

Wah.. ta - ho... ta - ho   Wah   ta - ho.. ta - ho Wah

ut ta ho na-wi tan a lo wah ut ta ho ta hi man a lo Ma ya

na wi zu mi teth la ni Ma ya na wi zu mi ta na li

Carlos Troyer—Pub. by Theo. Presser Co., Phila.

Enter in procession six or eight Maidens, slowly, silently, to tom-tom beaten in slow six-part time by the leader or Medicine Man. They walk with eyes on the ground, arms straight down at their sides, relaxed. At the end of the procession is a very small boy or girl, bearing the Peace Pipe aloft horizontally, and held in two hands, palms up.

The Chief stands with folded arms as they file in and form a circle about the Fire—three (or four) on the Chief's left, three (or four) on his right, the Pipe-bearer near him on his right, the Medicine Man on his left, the Herald directly opposite him.

Song No. 39

Prayer of Warriors Before Smoking the Pipe (Omaha)

Wa-kon-da dha-ni ga dhe ke Wa-kon-da dha-ni ga dhe ke Wa-

kon-da dha-ni ga dhe ke E-ha dha-ni hin-ga we-dho he dho

Alice C. Fletcher—27th Ann. Rep. Bur. Eth., pp. 464-65.

The Maidens sing the PRAYER OF THE WARRIORS BEFORE SMOKING THE PIPE (Song No. 39), hands held low forward, palms up, then raised high, palms facing in, for the first line; hands slowly lowered, then crossed on breast for second line; hands forward in beseeching attitude for third line; raised high, then arms folded, for the fourth line. The head is thrown back until the end of the last line as the arms are folded, when the eyes are cast upon the ground.

The Chief takes the Pipe from the Bearer. The Maidens sit down, cross-legged and cross-armed, in the places where they stood, and the Chief proceeds.

Kneeling at the Fire, he lights the Pipe. As soon as it is going, he lifts it, grasped in both hands, with the stem toward the sky, saying:

"To Wakonda, the one Great Spirit; that his wisdom be with us. Hay-oon-kee-ya. Noon-way."

All answer, in a long intonation, and slightly raising the flat right hand: "Noon-way." (Amen, or this is our prayer.)

Chief (pointing stem to earth): "To Maka-Ina, Mother Earth, that she send us food. Hay-oon-kee-ya. Noon-way."

All (as before): "Noon-way."

Chief (blowing smoke and pointing stem to West): "To Weeyo-peeata, the Sunset Wind, that he come not in his strength upon us."

Chief (blowing smoke and pointing stem to North): "To Wazi-yata, the Winter Wind, that he harm us not with his cold."

Chief (blowing smoke and pointing stem to East): "To Weeyo-hinyan-pata, the Sunrise Wind, that he trouble us not with his rain."

Chief (blowing smoke and pointing stem to South): "To Okaga, the

Hot Wind, that he strike us not with his fierce heat. Hay-oon-kee-oon-ee-ya-snee. Noon-way."

All (as before): "Noon-way."

Then the Chief holds the Pipe high, level in two hands, and proclaims:
"Wakan-tanka Wakan neekay-chin, chandee eeya pay-ya-wo."
(That is, Great Spirit, by this Pipe, the symbol of Peace, Council and Brotherhood, we ask thee to be with us, and take part in our Council.)

All intone a long "Noon-way."

The Maidens stand, the Chief hands the Pipe to the Bearer, who carries it high and marches off, followed by the others, singing the DANC-ING SONG (Song No. 40). The Herald leaves last of all.

Song No. 40
Dancing Song (Teton Sioux)

Frances Densmore—Teton Sioux Music, p. 145.

Sunrise Ceremony

The Herald walks slowly through camp, softly beating his tom-tom. As he passes each tepee door the second time, the inmates come forth and follow him, each wearing a blanket.

All proceed in silence to the Sunrise Hill. The soft thumping continues, until the first gleam of the sunrise. Then, led by the Herald, all sing the MORNING STAR (Song No. 41), "When the sun mounts, the day is illumed."

Song No. 41

The Morning Star (Ojibway)

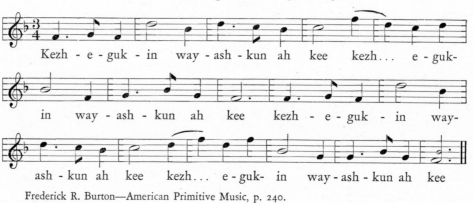

Kezh - e - guk - in way - ash - kun ah kee kezh... e - guk- in way - ash - kun ah kee kezh - e - guk - in way- ash - kun ah kee kezh... e - guk- in way - ash - kun ah kee

Frederick R. Burton—American Primitive Music, p. 240.

They repeat the song, getting louder and more jubilant, until the sun is wholly risen, when the drum stops dead, and the group returns to camp.

(I should suggest that on the last singing of the song, the final note be changed to the b-flat as notated.)

Thanks to Mother Earth

On a bright day, in the fullness of summer, all gather at a spot where a view of the country may be had.

Medicine Man

Behold! Our Mother Earth is lying here,
Behold! She giveth of her fruitfulness,
Truly, her power she giveth to us,
Give thanks to Mother Earth who lieth here!

All

We think of Mother Earth who lieth here;
We know she giveth of her fruitfulness.
Truly, her power she giveth to us,
Our thanks to Mother Earth who lieth here!

Medicine Man

Behold on Mother Earth the growing fields!
Behold the promise of her fruitfulness!
Truly, her power she giveth to us,
Give thanks to Mother Earth who lieth here!

All

We see on Mother Earth the growing fields,
We see the promise of her fruitfulness.
Truly, her power she giveth to us,
Our thanks to Mother Earth who lieth here!

Medicine Man

Behold on Mother Earth the spreading trees!
Behold the promise of her fruitfulness!
Truly, her power she giveth to us,
Give thanks to Mother Earth who lieth here!

All

We see on Mother Earth the spreading trees;
We see the promise of her fruitfulness.
Truly, her power she giveth to us,
Our thanks to Mother Earth who lieth here!

Medicine Man

Behold on Mother Earth the running streams!
Behold the promise of her fruitfulness!
Truly, her power she giveth to us,
Give thanks to Mother Earth who lieth here!

All

We see on Mother Earth the running streams;
We see the promise of her fruitfulness.
Truly, her power she giveth to us,
Our thanks to Mother Earth who lieth here!

(Alice C. Fletcher, *22nd Ann.
Rep., Bur. Eth.*, p. 335)

Thunder Ceremony

At the first peal of thunder, all hurry to the kiva, medicine lodge, or other central place of meeting, provided it has serious vibrations. The dining hall, for instance, would not be fitting.

The Medicine Man beats the time on his deepest-toned drum. This is done in rapid rhythm, and with sharp, loud thumps. The group, standing, and keeping time with stamping, sings: *

"Listen to the rumbling,
Listen to the rumbling,
Listen to the rumbling,
Listen to the rumbling!
Listen to the thunder,
Is it not the thunder?
Is it not the thunder?
Is it not the thunder?
Is it not the thunder?
No! No! No! No!

"Listen to the rumbling,
Listen to the rumbling,
Listen to the rumbling,
Listen to the rumbling,
Listen to the buffalo,
Is it not the buffalo?
Is it not the buffalo?
Is it not the buffalo?
Is it not the buffalo?
No! No! No! No!

"Listen to the rumbling,
Listen to the rumbling,
Listen to the rumbling,
Listen to the rumbling,
Is it not the mountain?
Heaving, moving mountain?
Is it not the mountain?

* The music is BEHOLD THE DAWN (Song No. 21), with the first half done three times, then finishing with the second half. The words are by Ernest Thompson Seton, and illustrate the Indian instinct to restrict themselves to few words in their songs. The original song had nothing to do with such a ceremony, but the rhythm suggested the words.

Heaving, moving mountain?
Is it not the mountain?
No! No! No! No!

"Listen to the rumbling,
Thunder of the rumbling,
Listen to the rumbling,
Thunder of the rumbling,
Red Cloud's war band,
Mighty myriads trample,
Red Cloud's war band,
Mighty myriads trample,
Ho! Ho! Ho! Ho!"

The song is repeated till the fury of the storm has spent itself.

Song of the Pleiades

The Pleiades are one of the interesting constellations of the winter months. Garrett P. Serviss says: "In every age and in every country, the Pleiades have been watched, admired, and wondered at, for they are visible from every inhabited land on the globe. To many, they are popularly known as the Seven Stars, although few persons can see more than six stars in the group with the unaided eye. . . . These seven were the fabled daughters of Atlas, or the Antlantides, whose names were Merope, Alcyone, Celæno, Electra, Taygeta, Asterope, and Maia. One of the stories connected with them is that Merope married a mortal, whereupon her star grew dim among her sisters. Another fable assures us that Electra, unable to endure the sight of the burning of Troy, hid her face in her hands, and so blotted her star from the sky. While we may smile at these stories, we cannot entirely disregard them, for they are intermingled with some of the richest literary treasures of the world, and they come to us, like some old keepsake, perfumed with the memory of a past age.

"The mythological history of the Pleiades is intensely interesting, too, because it is world-wide. They have impressed their mark, in one way or another, upon the habits, customs, traditions, language, and history of probably every nation. This is true of savage tribes as well as of great empires. The Pleiades furnish one of the principal links that appear to connect the beginnings of human history with that wonderful prehistoric past, where, as through a gulf of mist, we seem to perceive faintly the glow of a golden age beyond." (*Astronomy with an Opera Glass.*)

The Indians call them the "Seven Dancers." The legend they tell in this connection, I quote from Ernest Thompson Seton's *Book of Wood-craft*, pp. 209-10.

"Once there were seven little Indian boys, who used to take their bowls of succotash each night, and eat their suppers together on a mound outside the village. Six were about the same size, one was smaller than the rest; but he had a sweet voice, and knew many songs; so after supper the others would dance around the mound to his singing, and he marked time on his drum.

"When the frosty days of autumn were ending, and winter threatened to stop the nightly party, they said: 'Let us ask our parents for some venison, so we can have a grand feast and dance for the last time on the mound.'

"They asked, but all were refused. Each father said: 'When I was a little boy, I thought myself lucky to get even a pot of succotash, and never thought of asking for venison as well.'

"So the boys assembled at the mound. All were gloomy but the little singer, who said:

" 'Never mind, brothers! We shall feast without venison, and we shall be merry just the same, for I shall sing you a new song that will lighten your hearts.'

"First, he made each of them fasten on his head a little torch of birch bark, then he sat down in the middle and thumped away at his little drum, and sang:

> " 'Ki yi yi yah
> Ki yi yi yah'

"And faster

> " 'Ki yi yi yah
> Ki yi yi yah'

"And faster still, till now they were spinning round. Then

> " 'Ki yi yi yah
> Ki yi yi yah
> Whooooooooop!'

"They were fairly whirling now, and, as the singer gave his last whoop of the last dance on the mound, they and he went dancing over the tree-tops into the sky; light of heart and heels and head, they went; and their parents rushed out in time to see them go, but too late to stop them.

"And now you may see them every clear autumn night as winter draws near; you may see the little torches sparkling as they dance, the six around the little one in the middle. Of course, you can't hear his song, or even his drum, but you must remember he is a long way off now."

In the Pawnee ceremony of the Hako, there is a song to the Pleiades. Alice Fletcher has translated the songs, putting them into metrical form.

The following might be used on a night when the Pleiades are clear:

> "They come to us, they rise, behold!
> Over the marge of Mother Earth
> Into Father Sky, they rise, they rise
> Chakaa,* the silent brethren!
> Ah, 'tis a blessed thing to behold them yonder,
> More blessed yet for us to mount with them,
> To shine together each in his place as they!
> They come to us, they rise,
> We come to them, we rise,
> We as Chakaa mount on high!
> Behold them coming, climbing,
> And we as they,
> Brethren in unity together."

* Chakaa is the Pawnee name for the Pleiades.

The Naming Ceremony

The instinct to give nicknames is one of the deep-rooted impulses of the human race. In accordance with his wise policy of never crushing power, Ernest Thompson Seton long ago, in his work with the Woodcraft Indians, recognized this principle and enlisted its potency.

Through the ages, this practice of giving nicknames has persisted; but we have usually known them by a more dignified term than *nicknames*. Each new Pope, as he takes office, loses the name by which he has been known up to that time, and is thenceforth called Pius XIII or Leo IV, etc. The British government recognizes merit, and publicly does honor to it by a similar practice. In fact, Mr. Seton points out that America is the only country where nicknames are not officially recognized. To be sure, a number of them have at least helped to make their bearers famous, but they are given no official place in our social scheme.

Babe Ruth would lose the strength of his swat were he to be robbed of his title, and called Mr. Herman Ruth (I am not even sure that he *is* Herman). Thomas A. Edison has said that he prizes the nickname "Wizard of Orange" above any college degree that has been conferred on him.

Mr. Seton quotes a number of Bible characters who were given new names—Council Fire Names, as the Woodcrafters call them—and with them assumed new responsibilities. Abram became Abraham, Simon became Peter, Jacob became Israel, etc.

In our Woodcraft groups, a Council Fire Name is the last and highest honor which can be bestowed. It must be the unanimous desire of the group with which the chosen has been associated, is given only for a character or a career, and is done much in the manner of the Redman.

The ceremony which follows is based largely on Mr. Seton's ritual of naming; and, though the form is longer than the one he usually uses, it has been inspired wholly by his attitude and approach toward the subject.

The Ceremony

Fasting is an essential of clear vision, so that the candidate should abstain from meat diet for three days, and from all food (except water) for the meal before his vigil begins.

During this last day, each member of the associated group has made a prayer plume (Fig. 66). This is a slender rod of wood, the length measured from the inside of the elbow to the end of the middle finger. One end of the rod is sharpened to a point; at the other end is lashed a feather (or maybe a small bunch of feathers) with a wrapping of colored cotton cord. The rod is then painted according to the fancy of the maker. A good wish for the candidate is woven into the construction of each prayer plume.

On this night before the vigil, a brief council is held, to which each member brings his prayer plume. The Council is opened by the lighting of the Sacred Fire with the rubbing sticks, and the reciting of the twelve Woodcraft Laws in the ceremonial form.

Chief: "We are gathered here tonight with a serious purpose. We shall dispense with all frolic until after sunrise tomorrow.

"One of our number is to receive the highest honor in the gift of the Woodcraft Indians. It is the unanimous desire of this group that Charles Peters be given the ceremonial, the Council Fire Name. In preparation for that honor, he must keep vigil in the Sacred Place. That means that he is taken from this Council Ring to the Vigil Rock, where he lights a fire, and, in silence, keeps it burning until sunrise tomorrow morning. He may neither eat nor sleep, read nor smoke, go far from his fire nor receive visitors. If so be that the Great Spirit has a message to deliver to him, it is on such a night that it comes."

Chief (turning to the candidate): "Charles Peters, are you prepared to keep your vigil?"

Candidate: "I am."

Chief: "Then let us go."

To the singing of the GHOST DANCE SONG (Song No. 42), the Medicine Man leads the way toward the Vigil Rock, where a fire has been laid beforehand. He is followed by the group, each carrying his prayer plume.

Song No. 42

Ghost Dance Song (Arapaho)

Ni ni ni tu bi.. na hu - hu Ni ni ni tu bi.. na hu.. hu

Ba ta hi.. na.. ni hu.. hu Ba ta hi... na... ni hu.. hu

Na hi na.. ni ha thi na Na hi na.. ni ha thi na

James Mooney—14th Ann. Rep. Bur. Eth., Pt. 2, p. 996.

At the end of the procession, come the Chief and the Chosen, the latter carrying his prayer plume and a torch which he has lighted from the Great Central Fire.

In silence, all encircle the Vigil Fire, and the candidate lights it with his torch. He sticks his plume into the earth where it will be safe from the blaze, but within his vision.

The group plant their prayer plumes in the ground before them, each breathing a good wish for the candidate. Then they sing the OMAHA PRAYER (Song No. 42), with arms and faces uplifted till the last line, when they are lowered. The Medicine Man leads off in silence; the Chief is the last one to go, leaving the initiate alone with his prayer plume, his fire, and the Great Spirit.

Song No. 43

Omaha Prayer

Alice C. Fletcher—27th Ann. Rep. Bur. Eth., p. 130.

At daybreak the next morning, the group, in strict silence which has been maintained since the Council of last night, assemble at the Council Ring, where a fire has been previously lighted by the Medicine Man. They are seated till the Medicine Man approaches with the initiate. At their entrance, all rise. He is conducted to the fire, opposite and facing the Chief.

The Chief, in a subdued voice, asks, "Have you kept your vigil?"

If the answer is affirmative, the Chief continues:

"Do you wish us to proceed with this Naming Ceremony?"

If the reply is again affirmative, the Chief takes from his medicine bag a strip of birch bark, saying:

"On this piece of birch bark are the nicknames which have hitherto belonged to Charles Peters. In the name of this Council, I commit them to the fire. (Places the strip on the flame.) They go up in smoke, and are known no more."

Then, taking from his bag another piece of birch bark, the Chief continues: "On this other piece of birch bark, I have written the name which this Council is bestowing on Charles Peters. (Here he tells what qualities in the initiate have been the outstanding reasons for the honor.) For these reasons, in the name of the Council, I give to Charles Peters the Indian name of Wanakoia, meaning ——. By this honorable nickname, and no other, will he be known among us as long as this group and this organization exist. Wanakoia, I greet you—I salute you."

The group file past, shake his hand, murmuring: "How kola, Wanakoia."

They pass out the exit of the Council Ring, and return to camp.

Sometime during the day, a messenger is sent to collect the prayer plumes, and return them to the owners.

A Council Fire Name is the copyrighted possession of the individual to whom it is given; it is recorded at Headquarters, and may not be repeated.

Dedication of a New House *

My dream house was finished. I had had the unusual privilege and opportunity of not only planning it in all its foolishments, but in helping with the actual manual labor of construction.

I had done my poor little best in digging the foundation; the hired laborers had thought me crazy to expend so much energy with so little visible result. I had laid the cornerstone of the building, I had scratched the skin from my fingers with the stones of the chimney and fireplace, I had put on the first trowels of stucco till my hands were raw with the burn of the lime, I had painted some of the less conspicuous walls, I had done my duty by the workmen when the bush went up.†

And now, the rubbish was all cleared away, the laborers had left for good, and the house was swept clean and bright.

Could I simply move in? After all the weeks of planning and building, could I just put in furniture and call it a home?

There was some missing link. There was a wordless want within me that, for a while, was baffling.

Then the answer came; and for others who will feel the same need, I give what we—I and one kindred spirit—did to satisfy our craving for a ritual, a form of dedication that would hallow the place and sanctify the labor of love that had reared it.

The Ceremony

The woman sweeps out the house with a wisp of grass; then, standing in the doorway, hands a shallow basket of corn meal out to the man.

He enters, and rubs a handful of the dry meal on the south doorway timber, as high as he can reach. Then, walking in the direction that the sun travels, he does the same on the main timber of the south wall of the house, then the west, then the north, then the east, and lastly on the north timber of the doorway. While making these gifts, he preserves a strict silence.

With a sweeping motion of his hand from left to right, he sprinkles the meal around the outer circumference of the floor, saying in low measured tone:

* Dr. Cosmos Mindeleff, in the *Seventeenth Annual Report* of the Bureau of Ethnology, has given the Navaho dedication of a house; I have used this in part for the ceremony as given.

† Among all European nations, it is the custom to decorate the highest point of a new building with a green bush. This is the recognized signal that now the workmen may celebrate with a libation supplied by the owner of the house.

"May the house wherein I dwell be blessed;
May good thoughts here possess me;
May my path of life be straight and true;
My dreams as here I lie be joyous;
All above, below, about me
May the house I love be hallowed."

He then sprinkles two or three handfuls out of the doorway, saying: "May this road of light lead good friends hither."

Now, with the rubbing sticks, he lights the first fire. As it blazes, he stands before it, and says: "As the Great Central Fire of all reaches out to the four corners of the earth, and kindles blazing lights, so at our sacred symbol Fire light we our lamps, one each for Beauty, Truth, Fortitude, and Love. (He lights four candles, and places them in a row on the hearth.) And while these lights are blazing bright, we know that we shall grow." (*Birch Bark Roll*, early editions.)

The woman approaches, sprinkles a handful of meal on the fire, and says in a subdued voice:

"May this Fire, the symbol of the All Above, be the Home Fire of my children and my children's children."

She then tosses a handful up the chimney, saying:

"May the four winds carry off our troubles, even as they do this sacred meal."

Now it is the privilege of the friends and neighbors to enter the new house. Each brings a branch or stick of wood, and says: "Let me add this fagot to your fire, in hope to make it brighter blaze."

Any form of festivity may follow, now that the serious part of the dedication has been accomplished.

The Dance into Manhood (or Womanhood)

In our highly practical way of life, we are neglecting a wonderful opportunity which all primitive peoples seem to appreciate. In most aboriginal races, there is a ritual of initiation into manhood or womanhood, which is enacted at puberty. We may not, in all cases, approve the exact form the ceremonies take, but the fact remains that these people are impressing ideas on the adolescent mind when it is most susceptible to all such. Incidentally, much of the evil meaning we connect with some of these rituals is read into them by our own interpretation; there is no such thought in the mind of the participants.

*   *   *

Light the Sacred Fire in the center of the circle, as usual, with the rubbing sticks. In a circle about four feet outside of this Central Fire, build eight smaller fires, but do not light them.

Enter the initiate, stripped to breech clout and moccasins if a boy; in native dress and headband if a girl.

He (or she) does a simple, rather slow dance about the Central Fire, using a three-point pivot step (see Fundamental Steps, No. 19, with three taps instead of five) (12 meas.). Song No. 44.

With Step No. 14, enter eight dancers, same sex as the initiate, and who have already passed through this ceremony. Each approaches the Central Fire with an easily kindled torch, lights it, then backs up to one of the eight fires. The initiate stands close to the Central Fire, on the side opposite to the Chief. He stands with hands relaxed at his sides. The eight dancers hold their blazing torches high in air, and rhythmically stamp in place   12 meas.

Song No. 44

First Initiation Song (Chippewa)

Wa-sin-don-di-na-wa ha ni-kan i na wa-sin-don-di-na-

wa ha ni.. kan i na wa sin-don-di-na-wa ha

ni-kan i na wa sin-don-di-na-wa ha ni-kan i na

Frances Densmore—Chippewa Music, p. 45.

The initiate sings THE GROUND TREMBLES (Song No. 45), "The ground trembles as I am about to enter; my heart fails me as I am about to enter."

Song No. 45

The Ground Trembles (Chippewa)

Nin-kjin-o-cka-na-ki wa pin-di-ge-yan nin-djin-o-cka-na-ki wa pin-di-ge-yan.. nin-djin-o-cka-na-ki wa pin-di-ge-yan he e he e ha ni da ya... nin-djin-o-cka-na-ki wa-pin-di-ge-yan nindjin-o-cka-na-kiwa pin-di-ge-yan... nin-djin-o-cka-na-ki wa-pin-di-ge-yan

Frances Densmore—Chippewa Music, p. 38.

The group, softly swaying their torches, sing in reply, I Am Raising Him Up (Song No. 46).

Song No. 46

I am Raising Him Up (Chippewa)

Hwe-na - gi - wi - na hwe-na - gi - wi - na . . .   wi - na - gi - wi - hi - na - hi-

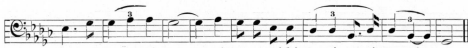

na wi - na - gi - wi - na . . .   wi - na - ga - wi - hi - na - gi - na wi - na - gi . . . na

Frances Densmore—Chippewa Music, p. 33.

Each kneels at his own fire and lights it from his torch, then stands in place.

The initiate now dances (with Sioux hop-step) about in a circle between the Central Fire and the line of eight lesser fires; while the group, still with the torches on high, progress sidewise in a circle (with step-lift-close, No. 2) the opposite direction from the initiate. They do this to the same song, I Am Raising Him Up   15 meas.

After one round, they twine in and out among the fires for one round, using the cross-toe-flat (No. 10)   15 meas.

They now stop. The leader advances to the initiate and starts the song We Now Receive (Song No. 47), "We now receive you into our midst, brother." He leads the initiate in to the Council Rock, where he is received by the Chief and given a seat. The others, still singing, exeunt.

Song No. 47

We Now Receive (Chippewa)

A - i - gwu gi - wi - mi - de - wi - i - go ni - kan a - i - gwu
gi - wi - mi - de - wi - i - go ni - kan a - i - gwu gi - wi - mi - de-
wi - i - go ni - kan a - i - gwn gi - wi - mi - de - wi - i - go ni - kan

Frances Densmore—Chippewa Music, p. 40.

PART THREE
INDIAN SONGS
AND
MUSIC

Indian Songs

Our reaction to Indian music seems to be universally the same, whether children or adults.

At first trial, we appear, none of us, to like the Indian songs. All their characteristics differ so wholly from our inherited notions of what songs should be, that the only impression we get is one of unrhythmic, unmelodious, untutored sounds, without rhyme or reason.

To be sure, we are all gripped—some more, some less—by the drum beat which invariably accompanies Indian songs, but the tune which underlies this is so exotic that it is disagreeable.

Soon, however—and with children much sooner than with adults— we begin to hear something under the pulse of the drum. What was at first mere unrelated tones, haphazardly thrown together, begins to emerge in a series of phrases which gradually take musical form in our ears; and we begin to listen with at least our minds, if not yet with our hearts. It is at this stage that we enjoy the beautiful lyrics of Cadman, Troyer, Lieurance, etc. At this time, also, we best appreciate the Ojibway songs recorded by Frederick R. Burton.

If we are fortunate enough to hear much of this native music, especially by the Indians themselves, we get to the third stage quickly. If not, the transition is slower, but just as sure at long last. The force of the primitive grips us, our minds fall into the groove once natural to us as a growing human race, we feel the impetus behind the songs, the untutored (if you like) but untrammeled evolution of expression, and we find ourselves wondering how we could ever have preferred the commonplace, cut-and-dried, balanced, inevitable form of our own modern music, in which we know at every point just what is coming next—mathematically correct, without variety of form, spontaneity, or inspirational urge.

* * * * *

There are many and good reasons to excuse our first distaste for Indian music, since our whole concept is so different from theirs.

Music and drama are so closely linked in the life of the Indian that it is often difficult to separate them. Music and dance are absolutely one and the same. Between music and poetry there is no line of division whatever.

The Indian's attitude toward singing is wholly subjective. It is "not an outer reflection of life, but an integral cause," as Hartley B. Alexander says of the Redman's art.

"Music, especially the rhythms of his drums, supplies his prime instrument of order. The drum commands life, and shapes creation; it unites times and dissolves spaces at will; it brings man into whatever communication his soul is set upon. . . . A function of the drum rhythm is to lift a man out of the exigent hour, and place him upon the hill of meditation or the mount of vision. . . .

"As his drum gives form, so his song gives substance to the Indian's understanding. This song is no artifice; it is art in that deeper meaning in which all true living is an art. It is an agent of communication, to be sure; but also of creation. For it is in song that he speaks across the abysms of chaos, addressing those Powers which move behind the screens of sense; and, if the song be potent, commanding them. . . . It is small wonder that the quest of new songs is a serious business of his life, and that, when found, they are prized and preserved as sacred Medicine."

* * * * *

The Redman never sings for the approval of an audience. One cannot conceive of an Indian on a stage, singing a composition to a packed house; nor an Indian as audience, passively listening to the beauties of such music. He does not sing and listen to songs; he lives them. His music is a means of accomplishing definite psychic results within himself or others whom he is trying to aid—nearly always to adjust human vibrations in accord with the Great Over-rhythm of the universe.

The Indian has a song for every occasion of his life, large or small, happy, sad or commonplace. Every event, every act, every activity, every phase of his daily life, every thought, indeed, may evoke a song. It must be this, in large measure, which accounts for the joy of life inherent in every Indian.

As a tiny babe, he is soothed by the rhythm of his mother's lullabies—mostly without words, though occasionally with an admonition similar to those we use in our own sleepy-time songs.

Song No. 48
Lullaby (Chippewa)

We we we we we we we we we
we we We we we we we we we we we we

Frances Densmore—Chippewa Music, p. 163.

Song No. 49
Lullaby (Zuni)

Dr. Frank Hamilton Cushing, used by Carlos Troyer, pub. by Theo. Presser Co., Phila.

Song No. 50
The Naked Bear (Ojibway)

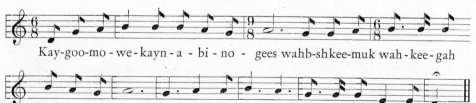

Kay-goo-mo - we-kayn - a - bi - no - gees wahb-shkee-muk wah - kee - gah

bi - da-quo - mig Kah kah - be-shees kos kos-kay-be-quay - ne - gen

Frederick R. Burton—American Primitive Music, p. 228.

A little later, in boyhood, he is engrossed with the games he plays with his own fellows, or watches his elders engaged in after the day's work. Each game has a song all its own.

Song No. 51

Song for the Game of "Hiding the Stone" (Omaha)

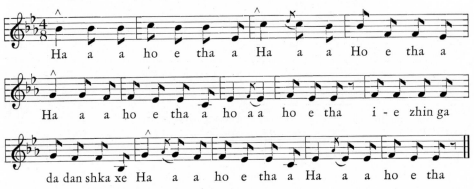

Ha a a ho e tha a Ha a a Ho e tha a

Ha a a ho e tha a ho a a ho e tha i - e zhin ga

da dan shka xe Ha a a ho e tha a Ha a a ho e tha

Alice C. Fletcher—27th Ann. Rep. Bur. Eth., p. 369.

Song No. 52

Paiute Gambling Song (Originally Mohave)

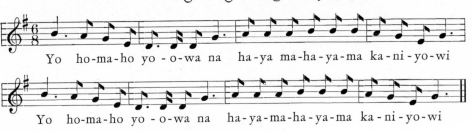

Yo ho-ma-ho yo - o-wa na ha-ya ma-ha-ya-ma ka-ni-yo-wi

Yo ho-ma-ho yo - o-wa na ha-ya-ma-ha-ya-ma ka-ni-yo-wi

James Mooney—14th Ann. Rep. Bur. Eth., p. 1009.

Song No. 53

Hand Game Song (Cheyenne)

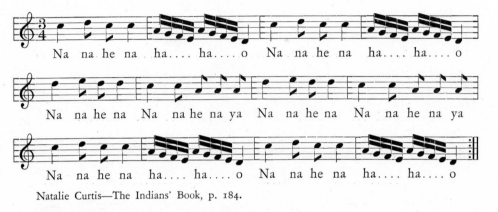

Na na he na ha.... ha.... o Na na he na ha.... ha.... o

Na na he na Na na he na ya Na na he na Na na he na ya

Na na he na ha.... ha.... o Na na he na ha.... ha.... o

Natalie Curtis—The Indians' Book, p. 184.

The young maid in the Southwest, in her 'dobe house, invites her friends for the day. As they help her to grind her corn, they sing to the rhythm. Often the village youths gather in the doorway, and add their voices or flutes in the sweet melody.

Song No. 54
Corn Grinding Song (Laguna)

Po... lai...... na,

Po - ho........ lai.... na, Hai - ke..... o.. tzi.. o....... no ho,

Ko - ho........... chi - ni... shi Ko............. esh.. Ka.....

si Hai - ke... o - tzi.. o...... no - ho ku.............

Ka - ni.. shi, ka.................. she..... shi, Hai - ke... o,

tzi o...... no ho, Ha - na - pu - ra - ni......... Po....

.... lai.... na, Po - ho.........

lai.... na, Hai - ke..... o - tzi - o...... no - ho Ha - na

pu - ra - ni......... He ye........ He ye!

Natalie Curtis—Indians' Book, pp. 466-68.

Butterflies, butterflies,
Now fly away to the blossoms,
Fly, blue-wing,
Fly, yellow-wing,
Now fly away to the blossoms,
Fly, red-wing,
Fly, white-wing,
Now fly away to the blossoms,
Butterflies, away!
Butterflies, butterflies,
Now fly away to the blossoms,
Butterflies, away!

A sick Indian, through all the ages, has known what our wisest doctors are now appreciating—the power of music on the tortured mind, with its gentle, healing reaction on the suffering body.

Song No. 55

Medicine Song (Navaho)

Notated by Julia M. Buttree from Victor Record 17635.

Song No. 56

A Midé Song of the Ojibway (No. 2)

Ni - ne - ta - we - he - wa wa-ba ma mani - do wa-wa - ba-ma man-i - do

Ni - ne - ta - we - he wa-wa - ba-ma man-i - do wa-wa-ba - ma man-i - do

Dr. W. J. Hoffman—7th Ann. Rep. Bur. Eth., p. 285.

Even the garments the Indian wears have personalities enough to inspire songs.

197

Song No. 28

Red Blanket (Ojibway)

Ay-quay-quog-nin-gah de - jah min   ne - ne-mo-shayn-nin-gah we - je - ah

Mis-koo - ah nin-gah-mah - jah - od wah-boy - on nin-gah-mah - je - dun

Frederick R. Burton—American Primitive Music, p. 210.

Of course, war songs formed a large part of the repertoire of every Indian. But "war song" meant so much more to the Redman than to us. A song of departure for the warpath, a song of meeting the enemy, a song of longing by those left at home, a prayer for the safe return of the warrior, an honor chant on his arrival, a recounting many years later of his prowess—all these ideas are embodied in the term. Even songs of peace and good will are so termed. The English translation of a number of these will illustrate: "He is the bravest of all men" (*American Primitive Music*, p. 258); "I am crying about my sweetheart who is fighting the enemy" (*ibid.*, p. 260); "I bid farewell to all my people as I go forth to battle" (*ibid.*, p. 261); "Inside the cave, that is where it seems my grandfather is" (*Chippewa Music*, p. 177).

Song No. 57

Inside the Cave (Chippewa)

A - pic-kwe - ka - mi-gaug-e   a - bi-dog - ni - mi - co-mis

Frances Densmore—Chippewa Music, p. 177.

Song No. 58
War Song (Navaho)

Notated by Julia M. Buttree from Victor Record 17635.

Honor chants or hero songs were much more common among the Redman than they are with us. We would do well to revive and create more along this line:

Song No. 59

Small-Legs (Ojibway)

Frederick R. Burton—American Primitive Music, p. 260.

"See that man with the small legs, the son of Always-flying; he is the best among us, for he is the bravest."

Song No. 4

Song of the Peace Pact (Chippewa)

E - hung - a...... e - hung - a Ga - ga - gins

o - gi - ma e - hung - a e - hung - a... e - hung - a

Frances Densmore—Chippewa Music II, p. 127.

"The leader, chief, is Little Crow." The song is continued *ad lib.*, introducing other names instead of Gagagins (Little Crow).

Song No. 60

Song of Triumph

Zon-zi-mon-de (Omaha)

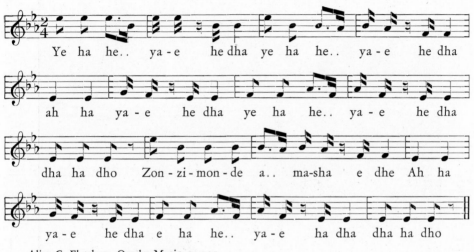

Ye ha he.. ya - e he dha ye ha he.. ya - e he dha

ah ha ya - e he dha ye ha he.. ya - e he dha

dha ha dho Zon - zi - mon - de a.. ma-sha e dhe Ah ha

ya - e he dha e ha he.. ya - e ha dha dha ha dho

Alice C. Fletcher—Omaha Music, p. 135.

The story which Alice Fletcher tells in connection with the above song is characteristic of the attitude of the Redman toward the aged. "Zan-zhe-mun-dae . . . was a very old man when the incident which gave birth to the song occurred. There had been an attack on the village, and the enemy had been driven off with such vigor that they were obliged to leave their slain on the field. As the warriors rode toward the dead to claim their honors, the old man, Zan-zhe-mun-dae, was seen coming as fast as his feebleness would allow; they halted for him to join them, and permitted him out of respect to his age and previous valiant career, to touch the dead, and thus carry off one of the coveted honors." (*A Study of Omaha Indian Music*, p. 49.)

* * *

In a measure—particularly in our childhood days—we have songs which approach the type of some of these, but the Indian meets even death with a song upon his lips.

Here, perhaps, is the basic difference between the attitude of the Red and the White man toward life. When the Indian knows that his time is coming to go upon the far journey, he does not crouch in a bed

75

76

Bear-Save-Life

Figs. 75, 76.

and beg for another year to live his life over again. He stands upon his feet, and with eyes upraised to his Father, sings his death song. Hartley Alexander has put truly the spirit of the Redman at this time into his

LAST SONG

"Let it be beautiful when I sing the last song—
Let it be day!

"I would stand upon my two feet, singing!
I would look upward with open eyes, singing!

"I would have the winds to envelop my body;
I would have the sun to shine upon my body;
The whole world I would have to make music with me!

"Let it be beautiful when thou wouldst slay me, O Shining One!
Let it be day when I sing the last song!"

*   *   *   *   *

The Indian has nothing which corresponds exactly to our popular songs. However, he has a great many social songs, sometimes accompanied by dancing. But, often, with no accessory other than the drum, singers will gather in groups and sing for hours, as we heard them at Cheyenne. Here a party of Sioux had come from Pine Ridge to add color to the celebration of Frontier Day. In the heart of the town, amid the traffic of the ever-present, rudely curious tourists, surrounded by the noisy, rowdy, cheap imitations of cowboys, the Indians were camped with their tepees. And here, as we too sought to avoid the janglement of the streets, we found groups of our Red friends in almost every tepee, quietly singing their songs, losing themselves in the harmony they were creating out of the discord about them. I think it was with conscious appreciation of our attitude that they graciously permitted us to stay with them.

*   *   *   *   *

One large class of songs are those prescribed by ritual and tradition to accompany specific ceremonies or dances. These are carefully learned by each succeeding generation, and are never altered in the slightest degree. If, by accident, one note, one syllable, one gesture, be wrongly given, the whole ceremony must begin again, or even may be abandoned.

*   *   *   *   *

I have heard it said that, among the old Indians, there were no love songs. Then along comes Frances Densmore with records of many love songs. She says, "Many of them have travelled far, and are known to be very old. They constitute a favorite form of music among the Chippewa." (*Chippewa Music*, p. 148.)
Alice Fletcher says the same of the Omaha.

Is it safe to say, "There are none of anything"? It might be more modestly accurate to say, "I have found none of these."

In our modern sense of the term, it is probably true that there were no love songs. The Indian knows how to leave a great deal unsaid; and, in regard to his deepest and most sacred feelings, can resist the temptation to rhyme *mountain* with *fountain*, and *love* with *dove*.

There are certainly a number of songs which approximate this class of music so common with us, but usually it is rather a song of yearning or parting.

Song No. 61

My Bark Canoe (Ojibway)

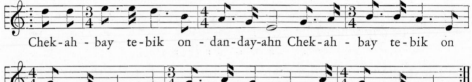

Chek-ah - bay te-bik on - dan-day-ahn Chek-ah - bay te-bik on dan - day-ahn ah - gah - mah si - bi on dan - day ahn

Frederick R. Burton—American Primitive Music, p. 203.

"Throughout the night I keep awake
Upon the river, I keep awake."

Song No. 62

I Am Going Away (Chippewa)

Frances Densmore—Chippewa Music, p. 183.

"I am going away. I pray you, let me go. I will soon return. Do
        not weep for me.
Behold, we will be very glad to meet each other when I return. Do
        not weep for me."

Song No. 63

Wioste Olowan—Love Song (Dakota)

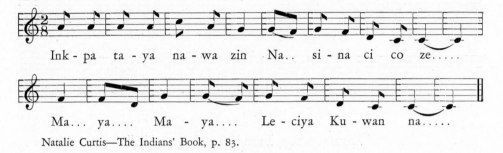

Ink - pa   ta - ya   na - wa zin   Na..   si - na ci   co   ze.....

Ma... ya....   Ma - ya....   Le - ciya   Ku - wan   na.....

Natalie Curtis—The Indians' Book, p. 83.

"Up the creek I stand and wave,
See, all alone I wave!
Ah, hither,
Ah, hither,
Haste thee to me!"

Song No. 64

Do Not Weep (Chippewa)

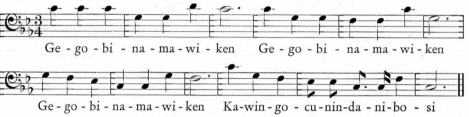

Ge - go - bi - na - ma - wi - ken   Ge - go - bi - na - ma - wi - ken

Ge - go - bi - na - ma - wi - ken   Ka - win - go - cu - nin - da - ni - bo - si

Frances Densmore—Chippewa Music, p. 152.

"Do not weep, I am not going to die."

There is one sweet little thing, of which Frances Densmore says: "This song is not without its humorous side. It is said that in the old times, an Indian maid would lie face down on the prairie for hours at a time, singing this song, the words of which are so very independent, and the music so forlorn." (*Chippewa Music*, p. 151.) Rev. William Brewster Humphrey has caught the spirit of this most admirably in his simple translation:

> "On the ground here I lie,
> Face to earth while I cry:
> 'That bad boy's naught to me,
> Why should I jealous be?
>
> " 'I care not, why should I?
> As for hours here I lie,
> That bad boy's naught to me,
> Why should I jealous be?' "

Song No. 65

Why Should I Be Jealous? (Chippewa)

Na - bi - sa   nin - do - ma   ge - o - den - da - ma - ban

ma - dja - kwi   wi - ja - sis   a   ya   ya   i   i   ya

Frances Densmore—Chippewa Music, p. 151.

Jean Allard Jeançon, in his article on the "Indians of the South-west," (*Pro Musica Quarterly*, June, 1927, p. 20) says: "The Indian has been accused of being a stoic and a bad lover. It has been my good fortune to see many young Indian couples during their courting and in after life, and I may unhesitatingly contradict such a statement. While their manner of courting is quite different from ours, yet there is much tenderness and love displayed during this period. The young man takes his flute and best blanket, and betakes himself to the near neighborhood of his beloved. Playing a beautiful yearning melody upon his flute, he strolls back and forth where the maiden can see him, and she slyly peeps from the corner of the window and watches him. Should she favor his suit, she at length comes out, and is received in the folds of his blanket, and the two stroll away into the darkness. Should he not possess a flute, he will sing to her softly, using the most poetical words that are at his command. In after years, he often uses the same courting songs to sing or play for his wife as they sit together to watch the sun go down, or in the house during the winter months of cold and snow. One of the most beautiful experiences that I have had was to sit with one of my sponsor-fathers and his lovely little wife, and listen to him sing love songs to her as the sun went down behind the mountains, and the cool dusk fell. Even after it was quite dark, she would nestle against his shoulder and listen to his voice as he called her his "Mountain Flower," his "Spirit Blossom," his "Little Wild Canary," and many other pet names. And the most interesting thing about it was that they had been married for more than forty years. It was not an unusual case. There are few divorces and little family friction among my Pueblos."

Mary Austin gives an incident which is mute evidence to this same thought. She says: "On one occasion in the high Sierras, I observed my

Indian packer going apart at a certain hour each day to shuffle rhythmically with his feet, and croon to himself. To my inquiry, he said it was a song which he had made, to be sung by himself and his wife when they were apart from one another. It had no words; it was just a song. Wherever they were, they turned each in the direction he supposed the other to be, when the sun was a bow-shot above the edge of the heavens, and sang together." (Introduction to *The Path of the Rainbow*, by G. W. Cronyn.)

There follows one flute call—the one which Cadman has used almost unchanged:

Song No. 66

Love Call (Omaha)

Alice C. Fletcher—27th Ann. Rep. Bur. Eth., p. 319.

✻   ✻   ✻   ✻   ✻

Songs are property, either of the tribe or of the individual. They may be bought, exchanged, or received as gifts; but even in such case, credit is always given to the original owner when used.

The Indian has, of course, no system of musical notation. But—and perhaps because of this—he has a remarkable musical memory. One evening, in the summer of 1927, Pedro Nieto was at our camp near Santa Fe. In exchange for a tune which he was teaching me, I sang him a number of Indian songs from various tribes—in all, about a dozen. He showed little interest except in four, which were of the Southwest. There must have been a quality familiar to him in these, since I had not told him where any of them had originated and they were all new to him. As I finished each one of these four—and they were scattered through the lot—he asked me to write them down for him. In each case, I wrote only the words, and gave them to him. When he was leaving, I asked what he was going to do with those words. "Sing them," he replied, surprised at my stupidity. "But I have not written the music, only the words," I said. "No matter; I sing them."

The next day, incredulously telling Dr. Edgar L. Hewett of the incident, I was assured that in all probability Pedro could do so—and he was no better than the general run of the race.

On another occasion, we sang a song to Martin Vigil of Tesuque. Two years later, on visiting his home, his wife sang it back to us, almost exactly as we had given it to him.

Because of this facility in learning music, every Indian has a remarkable repertoire. It is not unusual for an individual to be able to sing correctly several hundreds of songs.

As a rule, also, they are excellent improvisers.

✻   ✻   ✻   ✻   ✻

The Indian songs are practically all very short. Twenty-four measures is a long musical sentence; but this may be repeated over and over again, until one would think it would become monotonous. Yet, strange to say, this is rarely the case; the repetition enhances the charm, and we find ourselves listening for the familiar phrases with increased pleasure at each recurrence.

Song No. 67

Ghost Dance Song (Arapaho)

A.. ni qu ne cha wu.. na.. ni A.. ni qu ne cha wu.. na.. ni

A wa wa bi qua na ka.. ye na A wa wa bi qua na ka.. ye na

I ya huh ni bi thi ti I ya huh ni bi thi ti

James Mooney—14th Ann. Rep. Bur. Eth., Part 2, p. 977.

* * * * *

The question of intervals, tones, and scales has been discussed by every writer on the subject of Indian music. Does he use our diatonic scale? Has he a five-toned scale of his own? How many of these five-toned scales has he? Does he sing in quarter-tones?

Perhaps Alice Fletcher has best expressed the fact. "The Indian sings with all his force," she says, "being intent on expressing the fervor of his emotion, and having no conception of an objective presentation of music. The straining of the voice injures its tone quality; stress sharpens a note, sentiment flattens it, and continual *portamento* blurs the outline of the melody." (*Handbook of American Indians*, pp. 959-60.) Therefore, a piano gives only an inaccurate, charmless approximation of the real thing.

There is no part singing among the Indians, and their songs cannot be harmonized without sacrificing much of their innate charm. Simplicity is the keynote to their rendition. Let us keep it so.

* * * * *

As to Indian rhythm, here again is a moot subject. But why need we decide whether his use of rhythm is more advanced than ours, or less so? Is it not enough that it is different, therefore interesting and worthy of study?

The monotony of the rhythm of our songs stands out in contrast to the Indian treatment. If we start a song in three-part time, we feel bound to carry that tempo throughout the song—or at least till a definite number of phrases complete our musical sentence. Once in a while, in a spirit of adventure, we will switch upon entering the chorus of a song, but that is the limit of our daring, and is a recent departure.

Is the Indian hampered by any such conventional rules? No, indeed. His first measure may be 4/4, his second 3/4, his third 4/4, then perhaps a couple in 5/4 or even 7/4. He sings what the impulse tells him to sing, not what the arithmetic book says he ought to sing.

At first, the frequent changes of measure lengths, the accents unevenly spaced, disturb our smug sense of orderliness; but soon we find ourselves unconsciously losing the desire to accent the first note of each measure, and then we fall easily into the inner meaning of the music, and presently we are soothed and charmed by the infinite, soft, unhampered variation of the melody beats.

Song No. 68

Dsichl Biyin—Mountain Song (Navaho)

Hi ne ya Pi - ki yo... ye Pi - ki yo...... ye

Pi - ki yo..... ye Pi - ki i - ya Pi - ki

ya ya Pi - ki yo ye! Dsichl nant -i tai... Pi - ki

yo...... ye Sa - a na rai.. Pi - ki yo...... ye

Bi - ke ho- zho - ni Pi - ki yo..... ye Tso - ya -shich

ni la.. Pi - ki i - ya Pi - ki ya ha ko- la ra ne

Natalie Curtis—The Indians' Book, pp. 375-76.

Song No. 69

The Sky Replies (Chippewa)

Frances Densmore—Chippewa Music, p. 180.

"The blue overhanging sky answers me back."

There is one peculiarity which is, perhaps, the hardest for us to grasp, the most difficult to comprehend, and certainly the strangest for us to imitate. Each ceremony or act has its own rhythm of music, but not necessarily of drum beat. An Indian song may be a little faster or a little slower than the accompanying drum—or even in a wholly different rhythm. Alice Fletcher says a melody is often "confused by voice pulsations, making a rhythm within a rhythm, another complication being added when the drum is beaten to a measure different from that of the song; so that one may hear three rhythms, two of them contesting, sometimes with syncopation, yet resulting in a well-built whole." (*Handbook of American Indians*, p. 960.) Miss Fletcher, however, gives an illuminating note in the statement that "the beat governs the bodily movements; the song voices the emotion of the appeal." (*Ibid.*, p. 959.)

There is a syncopation in many of the Indian songs, which makes them a little more difficult to learn, but again avoids the monotony of the continually accented first count to each measure. This frequent use of a short note on the drum beat or emphatic portion of the measure is common to ancient Scottish music, and to much of our modern jazz. Is not this latter an unconscious groping after primitive expression?

Song No. 39

Prayer of Warriors Before Smoking the Pipe (Omaha)

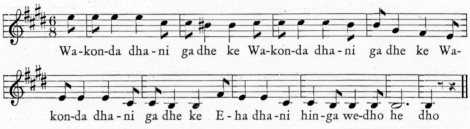

Wa-kon-da dha-ni ga dhe ke Wa-kon-da dha-ni ga dhe ke Wa-

kon-da dha-ni ga dhe ke E-ha dha-ni hin-ga we-dho he dho

Alice C. Fletcher—27th Ann. Rep. Bur. Eth., pp. 464-65.

This song represents also the characteristic downward trend of most Indian songs. We add one other such, from innumerable examples:

Song No. 70

Gomda Daagya–Wind Song (Kiowa)

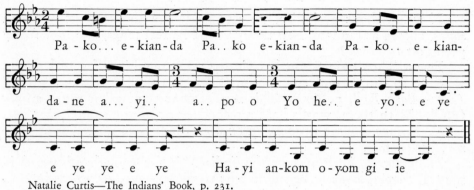

Pa - ko... e - kian - da   Pa.. ko   e - kian - da   Pa - ko.. e - kian -

da - ne   a... yi..   a.. po   o   Yo   he..   e   yo..   e   ye

e   ye   ye   e   ye   Ha - yi   an - kom   o - yom   gi - ie

Natalie Curtis—The Indians' Book, p. 231.

A fairly general form also is to start on a high note, gradually descend till the satisfaction of the low tone is reached; then abruptly start again on a high note, and drop again. The second half is usually a slight variation of the first.

Song No. 30

A Midé Song of the Ojibway

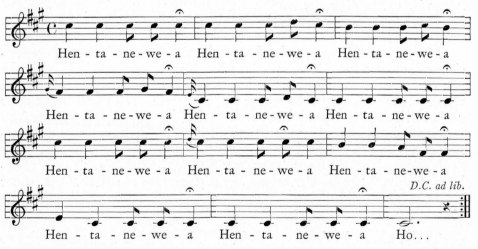

Hen - ta - ne - we - a   Hen - ta - ne - we - a   Hen - ta - ne - we - a

Hen - ta - ne - we - a   Hen - ta - ne - we - a   Hen - ta - ne - we - a

Hen - ta - ne - we - a   Hen - ta - ne - we - a   Hen - ta - ne - we - a

Hen - ta - ne - we - a   Hen - ta - ne - we - a   Ho...

Dr. W. J. Hoffman—7th Ann. Rep. Bur. Eth., p. 286.

The tone production of the Indian in singing is peculiar to the race. They sing with the lips almost motionless and teeth slightly separated. The tone is forced outward by the muscles of the throat, giving the voice remarkable carrying power.

Though their throats and speaking voices are normal, they use a falsetto in most of their singing. This is probably a ceremonial requirement. They cultivate a *vibrato* as an essential of the best singing; and often a nasal tone is employed, especially in their love songs.

*   *   *   *   *

If we, without prejudice, were to analyze a thousand of our own songs, chosen at random, how many would be real songs, and how many poems set to music?

Ernest Thompson Seton has given as one requisite of a real song a wording so simple and spontaneous "that it can live without print." (*Birch Bark Roll*, p. 60.) This requirement the Indian songs amply fulfill. With them, words hold a secondary or unimportant place in a song. In fact, a large proportion of their songs have no words at all— merely vocables.

Frederick R. Burton says the Indian "is far enough advanced in musical development to be indifferent to the presence of words in connection with his art." (*American Primitive Music*, p. 123.)

It has been said that the Indian in his song is content with a single thought. This is not strictly true; but he *is* content with a single expression—that is, the expression in words of a single thought. However, within that statement, there is what Burton has well called "compactness."

Natalie Curtis says: "One word may be the symbol of a complete idea that in English would need a whole sentence for its expression. Even those who know the language may not understand the songs unless they know what meaning lies behind the symbolic words." (*The Indians' Book*, p. xxv.) The connotation of the thought may be as broad as the compass of his life.

Mary Austin has marvelously caught this quality in her re-expressions of Indian verse (*The American Rhythm*). Merely to translate the words would be meaningless; but to get inside the thought and behind the impulse that created the words, as she has, then render them into our more obvious terms, yet without sacrificing the poetry, is to enter into a new world of sympathy with the Redman, and to experience a broadness of vision not attained by many White men.

The words of the song, THE SKY REPLIES, Song No. 69, are translated simply, "The blue overhanging sky answers me back." Another example is the following:

"Magic moccasins I am using."

Truly, as one Indian has put it, "White man's songs, they talk too much."

Musical Instruments

A list of the Redman's musical instruments would be very short, but the varieties within each class are many.

They are, of course, of two main types: wind and percussion. Let us take up the latter first.

Almost certainly, a skin laid on the ground and beaten with sticks was the earliest stage in the development of the drum. At Gallup, where we saw fragments of a number of the old dances, this method was used in several. (See Bow and Arrow Dance of Jemez, p. 35.)

The old Chippewa used to stretch a skin over stakes stuck upright in the ground.

The Utes used a hide in a number of special songs. Frances Densmore says: "Concerning the preparation of the rawhide used with the Ute songs, it was said that two large buffalo hides were sewed together and allowed to dry, so that they were very stiff. Holes were cut at intervals along the edge, and a thong passed through the holes. Both men and women stood around the rawhide, holding the thong with the left hand, and pounding the rawhide with a stick held in the right hand. Often ten or twelve persons stood around the rawhide." (*Northern Ute Music*, p. 190.)

Among certain tribes a basket is inverted on the ground, and beaten either with the hands or with sticks.

Sometimes a pole or plank is pounded with a short stick. On the Northwest Coast, a plank or box usually serves as a drum.

The hand drum, or tom-tom, is of general distribution, being especially adapted to solo work, and easily carried about from place to place. It is a frame of any desired size, covered with either one or two heads, though the one-sided tom-tom is more extensively used. In this type of drum there is always a hand-hold provided. Among the Chippewa, where the double-headed tom-tom is preferred, there is a loop fastened at one side, the drum being held suspended in air. In the one-sided type, there is a hand-hold at the back, of thongs passed through the edges of the head, or of the ends of the head itself tied together. (See B of Fig. 77.)

The old Hidatsa used a hide stretched over a turtle shell. The Eskimos of Western Alaska make their drum heads of the bladders of seal or walrus. The hand-hold, in this case, is an attached handle, four to six inches long, and may be a rod of ivory, deerhorn, or bone, usually carved. Among these Indians—and these alone so far as I can find out—the drum is struck so that the thumper strikes against the frame as well as the cover.

A tom-tom is always tuned at the fire before using it; and is the special possession of the owner, jealously guarded and reverently kept.

The larger war drum (tombé) has the advantage of a deeper tone, and usually some device by which it may be tuned. It is preferably a hollowed-out section of a tree—in the Southwest, a cottonwood. It is double-headed, with a loop attached at the side near each head. The two heads invariably have different tones. (See C of Fig. 77.)

In many cases, these drums are very large—sometimes several feet across—and are suspended on a frame of stakes placed in the ground; and, of course, in the true spirit of the Redman, decorated symbolically. A group of drummers seated about this provide inspiration for many hours of song and dance. (See A of Fig. 77.)

Unless suspended, either within a frame such as mentioned above, or held up from the ground by the loop—a hung drum—there is no boom to the drum—no musical tone, no spiritual uplift; nothing but an earthy, flat, dead thud, without vibration.

There is one other form of drum, perhaps the most musical form. A hollowed log, with a hide, dressed or undressed, for head, has a hole in one side, a little above the middle. Into this, water is poured until the desired tone is obtained. The tuning also is done by splashing the head with the water inside. (See D of Fig. 77.)

The drum stick, or thumper, for tom-tom or drum, comes in for its proper share of attention. The head may be hard or soft, according to its purpose, and may be loose at the joint, or the stick may go all the way into the covering. Again, in some tribes, there is no covering at all, the stick ending in a little ball of wood. The handle may be straight, or curved near the striking end.

Sometimes the thumper is a loop of willow or other pliable wood.

In our own work with Indian instruments, we use a softer thumper for singing than to accompany the dancers, though this made little difference to the Indian since he did not sing for an audience and could hear his own melody through any amount of loud beating. We also thin the handle a trifle where the thumb and forefinger rest, giving a better hold and easier swing; but care must be taken here to get the proper spot so the balance will be perfect. The Iroquois did this also.

Of course, the stick is decorated with painted designs. Streamers of ribbon or horsehair, or little bands of fluff around the stick at convenient intervals, add to the picturesqueness.

Rattles among the Indians are many and varied. The first type is a container enclosing small objects that hit together. The container may be a gourd (see E and G), rawhide sewed into a bag-shape and dried (see F and H), a cylinder of birch bark, a tortoise shell (see I), or even a tin spice box. These are filled with small pebbles, shot, or sand, according to the kind of sound desired. The amount of filler, rather than the character, determines the intensity.

The second type of rattle is a stick with small objects hung from it, so they clash together when shaken. These suspended rattles are made in different tribes of the dew-claws, or triangular pieces of deer hoof, birds' beaks, elk teeth, pods, shells, or tiny tinkles shaped out of metal.

There is another form of rattle, called variously notched stick, scraping stick, or *morache*. In some tribes, the jaw bone of a horse or mule with the teeth in is used. Others cut notches in a long stick (see K). In either case, the irregularities of the instrument are scraped with a smaller paddle-shaped piece (see L)—the scapula of an animal, or a slice of wood of convenient form. Almost always with this instrument there is used a resonator, such as an inverted basket on the ground, or half a gourd, or sometimes a plank laid across a ditch dug in the earth. The end of the *morache* is rested on this resonator, and the scapula drawn up and down it, the down stroke harder and sharper than the up, but in rhythm as a drum would be.

In the Northwest, the Indians use wooden clappers as rattles, but this seems to be a local custom.

Usually the rattle is held in the hand, but in the Southwest particularly there is often one tied to the dancer's leg below the knee.

Strings of bells, I suppose, must be considered among the musical instruments. In the early days, the bells were of hoofs of animals, each with a little clapper within. Now, however, ordinary sleigh bells are popular. These are worn on various parts of the body—strung across from shoulder to hip, around the waist, down the outside of the leg, or garters of them below the knee. These necessarily conform in rhythm to the movements of the dance, while the other instruments may be played in a wholly different rhythm to that of the song.

Similarly, small metal tinkles, usually cone-shaped, are sewn to parts of the costume, close together, so they jingle with the movements of the dance.

The wind instruments are of two kinds—flutes and whistles.

The flute is generally a section of soft, straight-grained wood, cornstalk, or reed, with holes bored at uneven intervals along the length. It has no definite scale, and the notes of no two are exactly the same, each player constructing his flute according to the convenient placing of his own fingers. It is played by blowing into one end of it (see M).

The whistles have no stops, and are made of the wing bones of birds, the quills of large birds, or of wood or pottery (see N).

The rhombus, whizzer, or bullroarer is used in a number of dances, usually with a sacred significance. It is the prayer stick of the thunder; and is painted in symbolic designs. It is a narrow rectangular slat of wood, often lightning-riven, attached by one end to a cord which some-

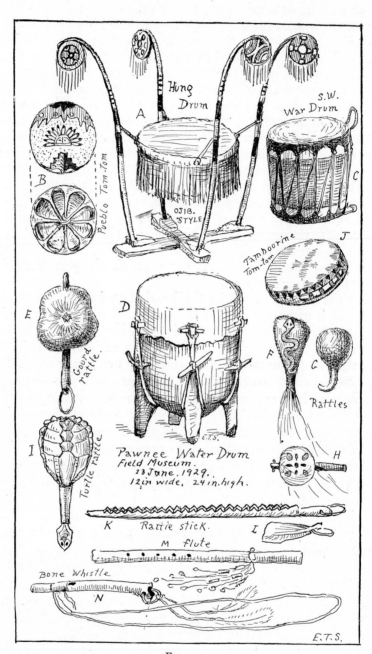

Fig. 77.

times is provided with a wooden handle. It is whirled rapidly about the head, creating a whizzing or roaring sound.

Stringed instruments are very rare among the Indians, the only examples being the musical bow of the Maidu of California and a few tribes in Mexico, and the Apache fiddle, which was probably adopted from the Mexicans, who use the violin to accompany their dances.

I have at home a corn grinder or mortar, made of a maple log, hollowed out at the upper end to a depth of about eighteen inches. The rim of this, when struck with a drum thumper, gives out a wonderfully vibrant musical sound. In the course of shrinkage, the rim has split into segments, each of which sounds a wholly different note. These are virtually a scale, though not with our intervals. I have never seen this employed by our Indians, but such a musical instrument has long been in use by the South Sea Islanders.

The Tom-tom Orchestra

An enumeration, or even a description, of the Indians' musical instruments would be of very little value in this connection, were it to end there. But the use to which we put them in our own work in camps and indoor meetings, makes it worth while to gather together this material from the various sources through which it is scattered—I almost said hidden, so difficult to obtain are most of these works.

To this end, we have in Woodcraft, what we call the Tom-tom Orchestra, though it has developed to such an extent as to include all the instruments available. I got the original idea from Mr. Edwin Pierce, of San Francisco, who had used a group of his Woodcraft boys, all beating tom-toms, in a parade of civic nature. Since then, our practice has grown into the following:

The tribe make as many of the instruments as possible; though we use also all the authentic things we have in our possession.

We seat our orchestra in a circle, in accordance with our Woodcraft custom. A large war drum, suspended on stakes driven into a frame, occupies the main position. About this, we seat four drummers, so arranged that all can see the conductor. Next to this we place our two cottonwood tombés from the Southwest; and one, made by ourselves, of a nail-keg, gayly decorated on both head and barrel.

The next group are the tom-tomers. We sometimes use in this as many as twelve or fourteen persons. Some of our tom-toms are tambourines, painted, with the tin jingles removed. Others are made of wooden chopping bowls, with two holes bored through the round back for finger-holds. Still others are made of boxes, round or even square; though the latter are not so good-looking. Where it has been impossible or difficult to obtain skin for the heads, we have used several thicknesses of brown wrapping paper, pasted together, thoroughly moistened, and allowed to dry after being fastened to the frame. These are not quite so resonant as those made of skin, but are a very good, inexpensive substitute.

Next might be used a dried skin prepared as the Utes did theirs (see p. 217). This would take care of perhaps half a dozen players.

The rattles may be as many in number as the industrious ingenuity of the performers allows. What with rawhide, wooden boxes, gourds, tin spice boxes, tinkles of metal, shells strung to a stick, and a score of other ideas, there is no end to the infinite variety of this department.

We have a separate group of notched sticks, using various types of resonators, and assuming different poses while playing. Some rest theirs on the ground in the position of a cello, some tuck one end under the chin like a violin, others with short sticks sit and rest them on one knee, striking them in the manner of a banjo.

In the bell department, we use one long string of sleigh bells, the two ends attached to a wooden frame, so the bells can be shaken with ease. Also, each performer wears a band of bells about either wrist and ankle.

The great value of the Tom-tom Orchestra lies in the fact that there is room for as many performers as one wishes. There is no doubt that one's enjoyment of a performance is assured if one be also an actor therein. I have seen a pathetic old spinster who had, all her life, been denied the gratification of self-expression, beam with joyous satisfaction when we put a rattle into her hand and had her timidly shake it in time to the song.

I add one song (No. 71) orchestrated for such a group as the above; and urge that the idea be tried out. It is sure to succeed, for psychology backs up the principle.

Song No. 71

Tawi Kuruks—Song of the Bear Society (Pawnee)

Notation by Natalie Curtis   Orchestration by Julia M. Buttree

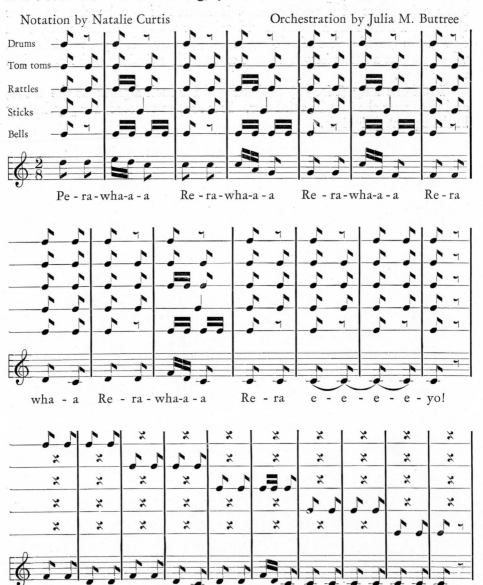

Drums
Tom toms
Rattles
Sticks
Bells

Pe - ra - wha - a - a   Re - ra - wha - a - a   Re - ra - wha - a - a   Re - ra

wha - a   Re - ra - wha - a - a   Re - ra   e - e - e - e - yo!

Pa - ra - ri - ku   ra - tu - ta - o   Re - ra - wha - a - a   Re - ra   e - e - e - e - yo!

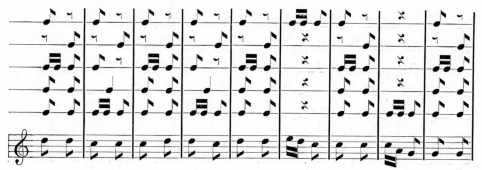

Hi tza-pat ra-ku-wa-ka-a ku-a-tu-tah i-ri-ri-tah Re-ra

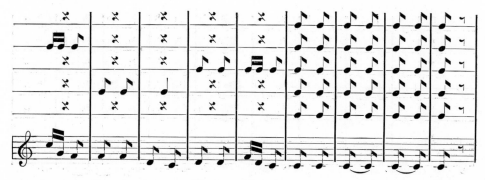

wha-a-a Re-ra ho... Re-ra wha-a-a Re-ra e-e-e-e-yo!

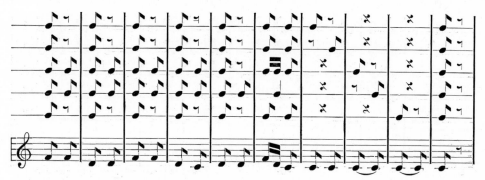

Pa-ra ri-ku ra-tu-ta-o Re-ra-wha-a-a Re-ra e-e-e-e-yo!

Ra - sa ku - ra ru-kuk sa - a Re - ra wha-a - a Re - ra wha-a - a Re - ra

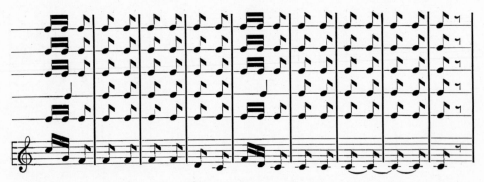

wha-a - a Re - ra ho... Re - ra wha-a - a Re - ra e - e - e - e - yo!

Ra - sa ku - ra ru - ra wha-a Re - ra wha-a - a Re - ra e - e - e - e - yo!

Natalie Curtis—The Indians' Book, pp. 117-119.

PART FOUR
INDIAN ART

Indian Graphic Art

By ERNEST THOMPSON SETON

To admire any special or well-marked school of art, and feel the desire to produce works of similar kind, presupposes a taste cultivated in that direction; for all of the well-known schools have developed artists of the highest merit, and no one can say that this or that is better. All he can say is that this or that school is more to his taste. Just so, a specialist in chrysanthemums cannot reasonably say to a specialist in orchids: "All chrysanthemums are better than all orchids," etc.

At best, one can claim only that each peculiar or national school has its own viewpoint or approach, and its own standards of excellence, as surely as each has evolved its own medium of expression.

Leaving sculpture for consideration in a later issue, the pictorial art of the North American Indian has these well-marked characteristics:

(a) It is, first of all and all the time, decorative. Although at times mnemonic as well as decorative, the beautification of weapon, tepee, or blanket was the motive thought.

The Italian masters made paintings that were to be seen as paintings only; that had relation to life and thought or religious emotion, but not necessarily to the wall of a house, the trappings of a saddle, or the fringe of a robe.

(b) The art of the Redman was never realistic, but always largely symbolic, and dealt in many conventional figures and designs that were not self-explanatory. He never painted the likeness of a buffalo, but always the symbol of a buffalo, with purely conventional symbols of life and sex added.

(c) The art of the Redman was extremely simple. It recognized only two dimensions; and was, in its purest presentation, at nearly the same stage as the Gobelin tapestries and Persian rugs of their earliest, unsophisticated—and best—era.

(d) The art of the Redman found its most joyful esthetic pleasure in color—not in form, not in line, not in groupings, but in color, more or less abstract.

* * * * *

The materials in which the Redman's art found expression were: paint on skin or wood or pottery; shell work; porcupine quills; sand paintings; engraving on metal or shell or wood. The nature of the material, with the traditional forms of decoration, imposed naturally the limits and characteristics of Indian art.

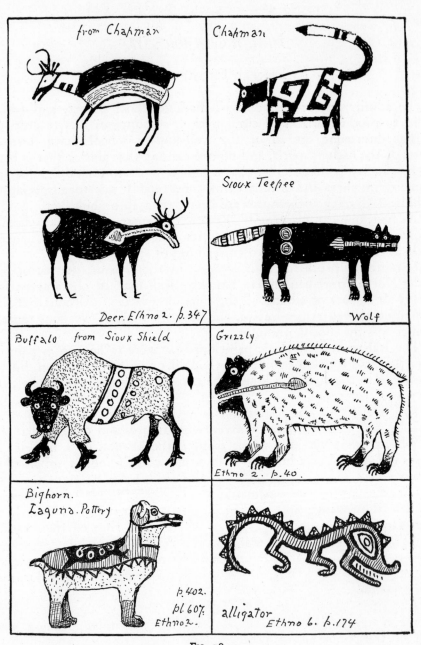

FIG. 78.

On account of its association with outdoor life in America, and its agreement with American traditions, as well as its artistic soundness, Indian art is at once turned to by those of our people who would go a-camping, and carry the atmosphere of the days of romance.

There are two well-known ways of acquiring the vocabulary of a new art. One is by following the motivating thought from the ground up, expressing it in the materials that were the original equipment of its artist; the other, the simpler method (and really the only one practical today for Indian art), is by copying good, authentic examples until you have acquired the style—mastered the vocabulary. These should be exactly copied, without variation, until the manner has been sufficiently acquired; otherwise, the danger of realistic violets tied with a beautiful pink ribbon, is apt to obtrude and do its poisonous work.

It is well to remember that examples may be ancient and authentic, yet not good; therefore, great care has been exercised to select specimens that are good art as well as authentic.

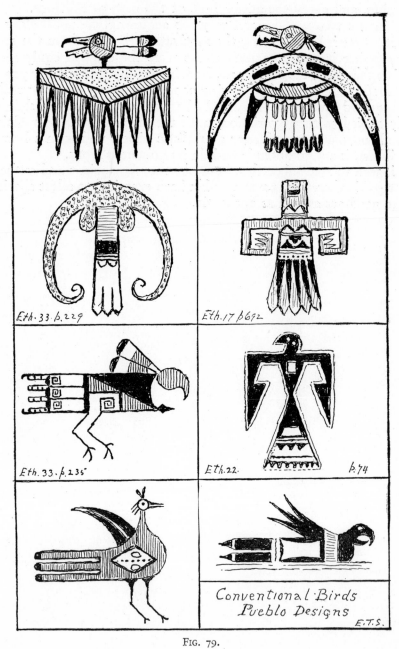

Eth. 33. p.229

Eth. 17 p692

Eth. 33. p.235

Eth. 22.

p.74

Conventional Birds
Pueblo Designs

E.T.S.

FIG. 79.

Making the Tepee

If you are possessed of the true spirit of Woodcraft, you will soon or late make your camp into an Indian Village—modified, no doubt, and equipped with several things not usually found in the primitive camp, but still colored with the picturesque ways, and dominated by the picturesque dwellings and decoration of the Indian.

The outstanding feature among these will doubtless be the tepee. The superlative advantages of the tepee are the open fire, the perfect ventilation, the warmth in cool weather, the coolth in warm weather, the lung balm and disinfectant supplied by the wood-smoke, and—maybe the strongest of all—its beauty and romance.

For general use in fine weather or in winter, especially in the West, we find the old Sioux tepee very satisfactory. Therefore, I shall first tell you how to make that, planning a 12-footer as a judicious middle size.

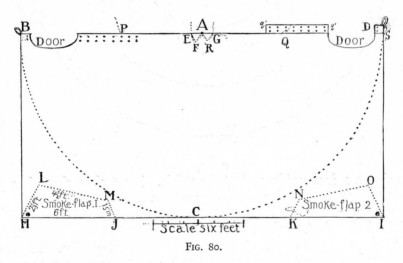

Fig. 80.

The original Indian tepee cover of old style was not a part of a true circle; was not even half a circle. This gave it more height and less width inside than the Woodcraft tepee which has been simplified into a true half circle; a change which results in its being easier to make and to manage.

Get 32 yards of 6-ounce duck (or heavier). Cut it into strips 8 yards long, run these together on a machine so as to form a square-cornered sheet 4 yards by 8 (BHIS). Lay this flat on the ground or floor. Then from a peg at A, with a string and a chalk, sketch the dotted half circle BCS (Fig. 80). Cut along this line, and hem the edge with a stout cord in it.

Cut out the two triangles AFE and ARG; also the two rounded pieces marked "door." From the scraps left, cut out the two smoke flaps as shown. Hem these, and stitch them on to the tepee cover, so that ON of smoke flap No. 2 is fast to GQ of the cover; and LM of No. 1 is fast to EP of the cover.

Cut a piece of canvas 4 feet long and 9 inches wide (when hemmed), and sew it on to the edge at Q (q' q'); and another 9 inches by 9 to sew on at DS.

Now, sew a peg-loop to the corner under each end by the door (B and S); and also one every 4 feet around the ground-line of the whole cover. These peg-loops may be of light rope, but are easier to sew on if made of canvas strips, each 18 inches long and made by folding the

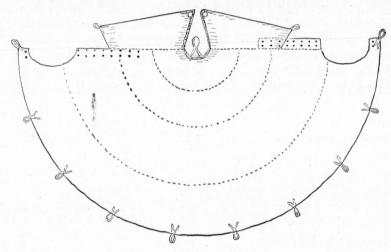

FIG. 81.

canvas about 1 inch wide and 3-ply thick. Note that there is a peg-loop at the bottom of each smoke flap; also at the central point A.

In the top corner of each smoke flap, make a 2-inch hole. These should be bound. On the edge at P and at q' q' are rows of holes punched through the cover. These are for the lacing pins. Those at P are supposed to fit exactly on those at Q, and those at B over the two at D.

An important reinforcement is a small rope sewn into the upper edge of the smoke flap No. 1, and extending across the cover to the top of smoke flap No. 2. Without this, the flaps will surely tear off soon or late.

The cover is now as in Fig. 81. The best and easiest time to paint it is now, as it lies on the ground.

Having made the cover, we need 12 lodge poles, each 14 feet long, straight and slender; and 2 smoke poles, each 16 feet long and even more slender; as well as 8 lacing pins and a dozen stout stakes.

The poles should be about 2½ inches thick at the base, and run out to about 1 inch thick at the top. If you are in a country where you can get lodge-pole pine, jack pine, cedar, spruce, or tamarac poles, slim and straight enough, you are lucky. Trim off all knots, all roughness, and all bark; and dry them out before using.

I have several times sent to a lumber yard for hop poles of the desired size. Many times I have gone into a thicket of soft maple or black birch saplings and cut the needed poles. But they are never very straight, and will surely rot in a few years.

I have seen bamboo poles used, but they must be tied very securely. They are too slippery for ordinary knots. Anyway, they are scarce, and not Indian.

Often, I have built my Indian Village of poles procured as follows: Go to the nearest lumber yard, select 6 pieces of 2 × 4 spruce, each 12 feet long, and one piece 14 feet long. They must be clear of all large knots. Have the millman rip each piece diagonally, so as to make of it 2 pieces 1½ inches thick at one end and 2½ at the other. Then, with a sharp drawknife, trim off the corners—and you have your poles, clean, white, straight, and seasoned. This method I have found particularly serviceable in the East where dressed lumber abounds, and poles are unknown.

The lacing pins, 8 in number, should be of any straight slender shoots —willow or arrowwood—15 inches long, a little thicker than a pencil, sharp at one end, and decorated, if you will, with rings of bark on the blunt end, or a tassel, or rings of red paint anywhere.

The pegs should be ordinary tent pegs, about 2 feet long, with a notch on one side near the top. There should also be one extra large heavy peg for an anchor.

The Setting Up

Now, we are ready to set up the tepee.

At a point 12 feet from their heavy ends, tie together 2 of the lodge poles, passing the rope once around. Then, on this, tie a third. (The Crows use 4 instead of 3.) An old squaw or a sailor could tie these so they would not slip; but it is wiser for the novice to drive a staple over the rope into each.

Measure a circle 12 feet across on the ground selected for the tepee and set up the tripod on this. Now set the rest of the lodge poles (except one—the lifting pole) as regularly as may be, in the forks, with their butts on the ground circle. Lash these together at the top by walking around outside with the long end of the rope two or three times, tying its end to the anchor stake which is driven down firmly inside the circle to the west of the center—that is, away from the door which always faces east.

Now, lay the cover down just west of the poles; and with inside upwards on that lay the last—the lifting pole. On this pole, 12 feet from the ground, tie the cover by the peg-loop A, at the top of the cover. With this pole, lift the cover up to place, carrying the two sides around till they meet at the east side, and overlap, permitting the lacing pins to go through, then out level through its mate; thus the canvas is laced together. (See Fig. 82.)

On each of the two long or smoke poles is a cross-piece of wood 6 inches long, nailed or lashed on at a point 18 inches from the top. Put the sharp end through the hole at the top of the smoke flap, till it rests on the cross-piece; the other end rests on the ground. A stout cord from the loop at the bottom corner of the smoke flap is needed at times to complete the adjustment.

Now, our tepee is up. It needs to be pegged down all round only in case of a storm.

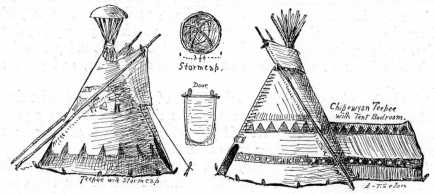

FIG. 82.

The fire is lighted in the middle. If the wind blows from the west, set both smoke flaps with the poles pointing east, and all the smoke will go out of the vent. If the wind changes to the south, drop the north smoke flap, and swing the south smoke pole till it points northeast, etc. If the wind blows from the east, close the smoke flaps on each other, leave the door open, and the smoke will be taken care of.

The entrance is closed with a door made of canvas on a frame, as shown. During the day this may be laid aside.

This is the old Sioux tepee—the lightest and most comfortable portable dwelling ever invented by man. It would have been used by all travelers in the West but for the difficulty of transporting the long poles.

The one weak spot is the smoke hole during heavy rain. To meet this we have the Mandan bullboat or storm cap. This is made of canvas on a willow frame, and is lifted into position by means of a long pole.

236

This requires a cover like that of the Sioux, but has no smoke flaps; and the whole of the portion above the topmost small circle (Fig. 81) is cut out. Its place is taken by a movable smoke flap on two poles as shown.

Further, the Chipewyan tepee has a bedroom or extension in the form of an A-tent tacked on. In one case I saw two of these annexes on the same tepee.

Since these side-rooms have a rain-tight roof, are wind-proof, often are provided with a mosquito curtain in front to make them fly-proof, and have the warmth and cheer of the open fire, they are the perfection of comfort for all weathers.

Painting the Tepee

The most conspicuous effort at painting that the Indian attempts—and perhaps his most characteristic—is the decoration of the tepee. It certainly adds more to the picturesqueness of the camp than any other painting that the ordinary camper can master.

Having constructed the tepee according to the directions in the previous chapter, it is ready for the painting. This is most easily done as the cover lies flat on the ground or floor.

The following paints I have found most useful:

Red. Red lead is the only beautiful red that will stand the weather. Also, it is inexpensive.

Blue, cobalt or ultramarine, lightened with white lead. These are beautiful blues, but no blue will stand the sun indefinitely; all fade in time.

Medium chrome *yellow*, *burnt umber*, chrome *green*, lamp *black*, and *white* lead complete the list. All of these, except the last, I prefer to have as dry powder, to be mixed as I need them with raw linseed oil and a little Japan dryer. Often a little kerosene is used with the oil, to thin the colors and reduce the expense.

Some like to keep the canvas of the tepee pure white as a background, on account of its beauty in the landscape and its lightness inside. Some prefer khaki. I have seen a beautiful tepee made by dipping the whole thing in red dye before it was painted with the designs. The fact that the dye takes unevenly only adds to the good effect.

To paint it, lay the cover flat on the floor—all the better if tacked down; find the exact point around which the half circle was drawn in making it. With a string held at this point, and a chalk at the proper distance, trace all the semicircles that are indicated, or are needed for guidance. Chalk is best for this, as it is easily washed off later—one shower of rain and it is gone.

With these semicircles as guides, now sketch in the animals, etc.

Two sizes of brush are needed—one about 2 inches wide for large areas; and one 1/4 inch wide for stripes, etc. When changing from one color to another, brushes should be washed clean with kerosene, turpentine, or hot soapy water.

The tepees in Fig. 83 are shown without smoke poles, pegs, etc., for the sake of simplicity.

In the first example, the Sioux tepee, most of the pattern is black on the buff ground of the leather. The star is blue, and each of the four wolves is black with red ankles, kidneys, and heart; also red and blue

Sioux.
Am. Mus

F. A. Verner's
Tepee.

Paul Kane
Red Bear
Tepee

Thunder Bull's
(Cheyenne)

E. T. Seton

bands on tail and on the life-line that goes down the throat. The black decoration at the bottom is supposed to be alternated trees and distant mountains. The light spots below are lakes, and may be buff or blue. On the smoke flaps are stars; these also may be buff or blue.

The second tepee was recorded by F. A. Verner of Toronto, Canada. It had a green chevron on the lower part. I do not know how authentic this was. The old Indians had neither green nor blue; and the best-looking tepees I have seen were painted in red, black, yellow, and white.

Paul Kane gives a sketch of a Red Bear tepee as shown. The only colors are the red band, out of which the red bear comes; and the buff color of the leather.

On the lowest and last tepee, the animals were flat brown tint; the line on which they stand with the medicine ladder, blue.

Thunder Bull's tepee, I bought from him some twenty-five years ago in Oklahoma. It was not painted, but decorated with beaded shields, from each of which hung three tassels of grass and horsehair. The four shields on the side were about six inches across; the big one up near the lifting strap was twelve inches wide.

This tepee was part of my Indian Village at Cos Cob in 1902. I lived in it off and on for years—till it rotted away and was replaced by those now in use.

The War Bonnet

The war bonnet of the Sioux is, in my opinion, the most gorgeously picturesque headdress ever invented by a primitive people. It is so superbly decorative, symbolic, and splendid, that it has spread, in the last fifty years, to nearly every Indian tribe. In all our allegorical art it has become the Redman's typical adornment, notwithstanding the fact that it was the last of the representative headgears to be discovered by the White explorers of this continent.

There are many varieties of the war bonnet, but experience shows that it is best to stick to the simplest design. I have seen many with bunches of ribbon at each ear; many with a medicine plume in the center; some with a tail that trailed on the ground except when the wearer was on horseback; some with two tails, some with no tail at all; some with a buffalo horn at each ear; some with strings of mirrors behind. But, in each and all, the central essential, typical and glorious thing dominant, was the sunburst of white eagle plumes.

Therefore, I shall describe the making of that, omitting the tail, the medicine plume, and the horns, etc.

Materials

We must assume that real eagle feathers are not available, the substitute being the "white quills" sold by all millinery supply houses (addresses of reliable firms can be had at the Woodcraft League of America, 1043 Grand Central Terminal Bldg., New York City) at a cost of about $1.00 a dozen. You will need thirty of these; and, since they are really from the wings of swans, etc., they should be half rights and half lefts.

Next, we need a quantity of white down. The entire product of a white Brahma's rear elevation would be about right. This may be used white, or dyed yellow or red.

We need further some thin leather, some fine linen thread, shoemaker's wax, a yellow or red dyed horsetail of the kind sold as harness hangers, and some thin red flannel.

Preparing the Feather

On the barrel of the feather, 2 inches from the bottom, lay on enough down to make a big fluffy ruff, then lash that on with a wax-end.

With real eagle feathers it was usual to cut away half of the quill for 1½ inches near the bottom, then bend the remaining half and thrust it into the barrel, to give a strong loop. But the swan feathers have less quill and must have a different attachment. This is made of a leather strap, 4 inches long and ⅛ inch wide, lashed on the barrel of the quill as in the sketch, with a waxed thread or wax-end. The quill itself should be rubbed with wax before the lashing goes on as this prevents slipping.

Over this leather, now stitch a cover of red flannel for a finish. Near the 2 ends of this wrapping, wind it with white cord, in a band wide enough to be easily visible at a distance.

The top end of the feather is to be decorated with a down tuft of the same color as that below. This may be glued on, but is better if it have also a thread lashing, and a helpful final touch is a white paper circle ¾ inch across glued on this.

Projecting above and beyond, if you desire it, is a tuft of yellow or red horsehair, 4 or 5 inches long, neatly lashed as before to the mid-rib of the quill.

Prepare the 30 quills all in the same way. I have seen the corona made of 24 quills—2 tails—but it looks skimpy unless you have real eagle tail feathers which are very broad.

The vast majority of war bonnets these days are founded on the crown of an old felt hat; but the primitive fashion is good enough, and is more enduring.

Make a strip of leather or buckskin, 23 inches long and 2½ inches wide. Sew this into a circle to fit your head just above the eyes and ears. Divide this along the middle line into 30 spaces; then at either side of each dividing line push 2 holes big enough for a lace.

Assembling the Crown

Lay the 30 plumes in a row, beginning in the middle with the largest, and selecting all the right feathers for the right side, etc., carefully changing them about till you have them best fitted to each other, and to the circle.

The leather circle should now be held on two fingers or two pegs, upside-down, while the feathers are strung on. Begin at the middle of the front, put the lace from the inside through a hole, through the leather loop of a plume, then back through the next hole; and so on, doing the 15 on one side, then the 15 on the other, again beginning at the middle of the front.

The spacing string is next, and calls for some very deft handling. This is a linen thread well waxed, which is passed with a needle through the mid-rib of each quill at half its height. It must go through the whole 30 feathers, and its ends be tied loosely together. The feathers must now be evenly adjusted, so as to form the perfect cone-shape, the feathers flaring out in a circle about 20 inches in diameter. If more than that, the crown is over-spread at the points, and never keeps its

241

leather headband

Brow-bands

leather strip on Quill

red cloth wrapping

Finished feather

E. T. Seton

FIG. 84

shape; every puff of wind deranges it. If less than that, it looks like a stove-pipe hat.

The Decorations

There are three decorations that are never omitted in a complete war bonnet—the beaded brow-band, the ear targets, and the ear plumes.

The beaded brow-band or frontlet, extending across the brow, below the feather bases, should be chiefly white, and of very simple pattern, such as a line of tepees or of square blocks. Sometimes, this is painted when there is no time to bead it.

The ear targets should be round, much wider than the brow-band, chiefly white, and beaded or painted.

The ear plumes hang from a cord in the middle of the target, or else underneath it. I have seen feathers, bead strings, thongs, and ribbons used for these; but the ideal always has been ermine skins and tails, four on each side, and pulled out into long thin streamers. Real ermine is over-costly; but I have made a good imitation out of a strip of white rabbit fur, and finished off with a black tip of cat or skunk fur.

Moccasins

In my young days on the Plains of the North, we put on moccasins over three pairs of stockings at the end of October, and wore no other footgear till the early part of March. A possible exception to this was that each of us had a pair of rubbers that could be slipped over the moccasins when we had to do our daily task in the sloppy by-product of the stable.

Once in a while, there came amongst us an Easterner or a European who was determined to wear the same boots in the Northwest as he did in his Eastern home. He was usually in the hospital with frozen feet within a month.

Thus, the Indian moccasins, with their warmth, their foot play, and their perfect circulation, were an essential of comfort during five months of the year in all of the region that lies north of latitude forty-nine degrees.

In that country each of us had to stock up with moccasins or else make our own when winter drew near. So that the making of moccasins was as well known as the knitting of socks. All of us could do a little of it; most of us had mastered the subject.

This was the condition till the Mennonites came in, and introduced a new type of moccasin made of thick felt with a rubber sole. They were very comfortable, but very heavy; and are now commonly worn by all teamsters in the Northwest.

In our moccasin days there were two types well known: (1) the Ojibway or Pucker-top moccasin, with a soft sole, and soft uppers, made of buckskin leather; and (2) the Sioux type, which had a hard or raw-hide sole, because the people who originated it lived in a country abounding with cactus.

For the benefit of those who wish to make their own moccasins for Indian dancing, I give instructions as follows:

The Ojibway or Pucker-top Moccasin (Fig. 85)

This was usually made of three pieces, each a different kind of leather —the sole of the heaviest moosehide, the ankle flaps of thin, soft buckskin, and the inset or tongue of the finest caribou leather, elaborately decorated.

The Sole. Set your foot on a good thick piece of moose leather (A), and trace the outline of your foot as shown. Outside of this line, draw another, 2 inches from it, except in the middle where it is but 1½ inches away. At the heel the line is straight across with a little heel flap left on. Cut along this outer line—and your sole is ready.

The Ankle Flap or Uppers. These are of any soft leather; doeskin or antelope does quite well. The pattern is as shown in B, but the scale must be adapted to your own foot.

The Tongue or Inset. For the best moccasins this is usually made of fine white caribou leather embroidered with beads, quills, or silks (C). The embroidery is done, of course, before the tongue is sewn in. The sole may wear out, but the tongue does not. It is commonly removed from one pair of moccasins to another.

When rough-and-ready Ojibway moccasins are needed both of the pair are alike—there are no lefts or rights. But a fine pair of moccasins commonly has the tongues decidedly right and left—this gives a much more elegant and fitted appearance.

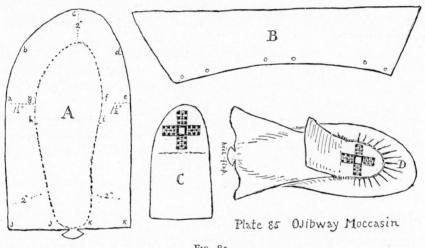

Plate 85 Ojibway Moccasin

Fig. 85.

The patterns in Fig. 85 were made for a foot 8 inches long. This fact must be kept in mind while making the patterns for your own foot. Keep the same ratio in all parts.

When ready to assemble your parts take a strong needle and heavy linen thread (unless you wish to work with sinew). Begin at A, and run a puckering string all around the edge (a, b, c, d, e), with a stitch every quarter of an inch: draw this string tight, adjust it carefully and evenly. Then your moccasin top will be as at D, with the tongue inset.

Insert the tongue or inset (as in D), stitch it onto the inner rim of the pucker, and an inch back of this on either side—that is, to (h) and (i).

Now, put the moccasin on your foot; draw JJ to KK at the heel to make sure of the fit; all adjustment is made at the heel seam. When these are right, close the seam and finish by sewing the heel flap up against the seam.

Next, stitch the ankle flaps B along the upper edge of the sole piece, sewing it on solidly from the heel along each side to the beginning of the pucker on each side of the front.

Run a 24-inch buckskin thong through the 6 holes shown in the base of the ankle flaps, making sure that at the heel end it is outside—and the moccasins are ready for use.

These Woodland moccasins are quite the best for the deep, dry snows of the Saskatchewan; but the arid, thorny, cactus-strewn plains of the Missouri call for a harder and more resistant make, represented by the footgear of the Sioux.

The Sioux or Hard-sole Moccasin (Fig. 86)

The chief peculiarity of this is the thick, hard sole, often made of rawhide.

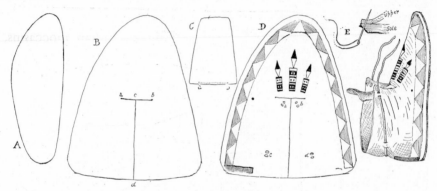

FIG. 86.

Sole. Set your foot in the selected piece of heavy leather or rawhide, and draw the outline. Cut it out as at A for the left foot, reversing the pattern for the right. Bevel the edge of this so as to get the form shown in E.

Upper. Now, cut the uppers out of soft leather, following the pattern B. This is an inch longer than A, but of the same width as the length of A at the widest part or bottom.

Any embroidery or ornamentation that is planned should be done on the upper at this time (D).

Make the two cuts dc and ab. Now, stitch the edges of the upper D to the edges of the sole A, as at E, beginning at the toe and working back to the heel on each side, leaving the closing of the heel till the last thing.

Sometimes, the moccasins are turned inside-out for this stitching. It makes a neater job but is not easy with a hard sole.

Tongue. The tongue, C, is of soft leather. It is sewn on to the upper at ab, but overlaps at each side so as to leave no opening. Sew up the heel, perforate for strings as shown, and the moccasin is ready.

This type of moccasin is always in rights and lefts.

An even more effective sole is made thus: Cut your rawhide ½ inch wider than your foot all around. Then make a board exactly the size of your foot, and about an inch thick, with rounded edges. Soak your sole till soft; then bend and hammer it on the board and up on the edges. Tack or bind it there till set and dry. Then take it off, and stitch to the uppers as already set forth. The upper is, of course, smaller with this larger sole. Oftentimes during work, the leather may be made more tractable by dampening it.

This Sioux style is more troublesome to make than the pucker-top; but it protects the foot better and keeps the stitching from wearing out against the ground. On the other hand, I often found that in severe winter weather the hard-sole moccasin gets unpleasantly smooth and slippery, as well as less stimulant of good foot circulation.

Moccasin Made of Sneaks

I have given instructions for the making of Indian moccasins, in strictly Indian fashion (Figs. 85 and 86). But we have found, in most of the Woodcraft camps, that it is easier, cheaper, and in the long run more satisfactory, to make your moccasins out of a pair of gym sneaks. These are sure to be comfortable, and adequately protect the feet. The cost of them complete is less than the buckskin alone would cost to make Indian moccasins.

In Fig. 87, I give a series of decorations that can be applied to the sneaks, either as paint, beads, silk embroidery, or appliqué.

Paint—that is, solid oil paint—is most easily and effectively used. A black outline in waterproof ink, or indelible pencil, is often very helpful to emphasize the pattern. It is assumed that the sneaks are either white or brown to begin with.

If you follow the directions on the Plate—that is, the colors indicated by the lines or dots—then actually color the Plate with water colors, you will get a much better idea of the effect.

No. 1 (A and B) is a design in red and white, painted on the tan color of the sneak.

No. 2 is red on a green ground, with white triangles at the side; and is most easily done on a white sneak.

No. 3 is on a white sneak, a design in red with blue center. The fringe is of leather, sewn on the outer edge of the opening; and may be much longer if desired.

No. 4 is a very simple pattern of red and white on the tan color of the sneak.

No. 5 is white chiefly—that is, it is a white sneak with a blue and white band near the sole, a red circle in front around which is a ring of pale green and rays of deep yellow or orange. I have seen this one done in embroidery of silk as well as painted.

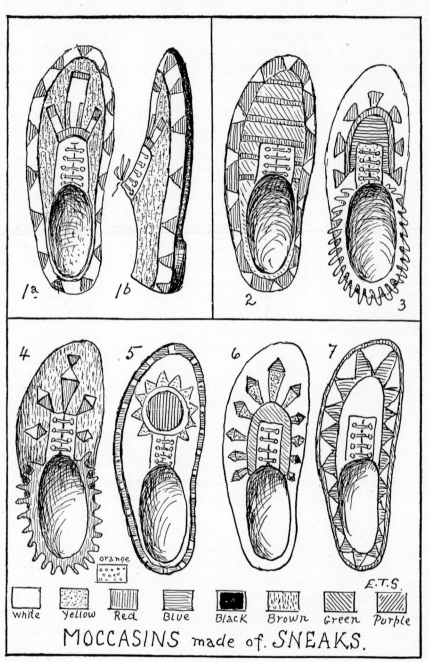

1a 1b 2 3

4 5 6 7

orange

white Yellow Red Blue Black Brown Green Purple

E.T.S.

MOCCASINS made of SNEAKS.

FIG. 87.

No. 6 is a white sneak with a green top, center and feather of deep yellow or orange, tipped with blue.

No. 7 also is a white sneak, with orange top, blue triangles, and a band of red all around next the sole.

All may be fringed if desired.

Almost any good Indian moccasin pattern may be reproduced in colors on a sneak; but the beginner especially is advised not to try original designs—at least, not until after a long course of exactly copying those made by Indians.

Breech Clouts

The typical Indian, during warm weather, wore but two garments: breech clout and moccasins. Already, these are the adopted costume in many summer camps and bathing resorts, especially with the very young.

At a camp recently visited, the councillors said, "We will adopt this costume if you will show us some good patterns with pretty decorations." In response to the needs of the camp, and of others like-minded, I give a series of practical designs.

A good breech clout is, first, a pair of very short pants, cut as in the sketch, with a buckle, button, or tie-strings at one side. It has, further, a decorated flap from the middle of the belt in front, and another from the middle of the belt behind.

There is little variation in the shorts, but the flaps and the belt may be changed by decoration to any extent.

A number of Indian designs are given in Fig. 88, but the emblem of the camp is always a good thing to add.

It is well, also, to make the flaps hang aright, by the addition of weights, such as shells, beadwork, or pieces of metal.

Most of the patterns shown can be rendered in appliqué of colored felts on the cotton or khaki of the garment.

Woodcraft Buttons

When you receive your Woodcraft honor band, you find that it has no button to secure it at the hip. The reason is that each member is supposed to make his own button, with something of his own personality in it.

I have before me such buttons made of wood, horn, bone, leather, shell, metal; one or two are antler tips of a deer's horn; one is a slice of the horn from the first deer that the man killed; one is an elk tooth; one a bear tooth; another a bear claw; one a flint arrowhead; one is a silver thunder bird; another a Mexican dollar; one a Japanese coin. All are fastened on with a thin buckskin thong.

A few are shown in Fig. 89.

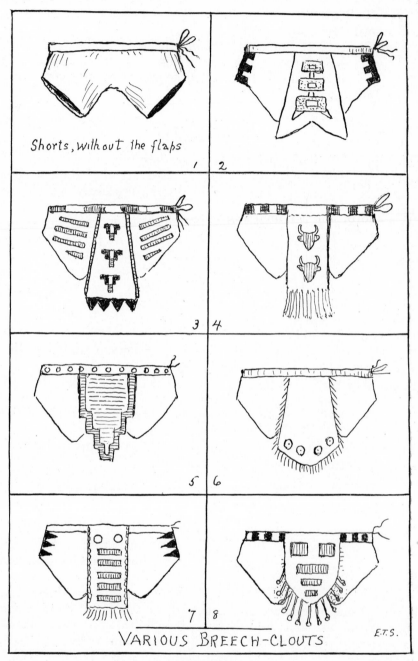

Shorts, without the flaps

1　2
3　4
5　6
7　8

VARIOUS BREECH-CLOUTS

E.T.S.

Fig. 88.

Making a Buffalo Skull

For the SUN DANCE, each dancer needs a buffalo skull. Real skulls are no longer at hand; but we can make wooden skulls that look very well, and have the advantage of being much lighter.

Once, under challenge, I made a skull complete in twenty minutes; but I prefer to spend an hour or more over each.

Take a block of spruce, pine, or other soft wood, 10 inches thick, 15 inches long, with no large knots. Split it down the center.

Take one-half, remove the bark, smooth it, and sketch on it the form shown in Fig. 89.

At a and b, sink a 1-inch auger hole about 2 inches deep. At c and d, sink a 2-inch auger hole about 2 inches deep.

Now take a sharp hatchet or drawknife, and trim the block along the dotted lines, until the skull is like Fig. 89.

Cut a hole through the palate, that is, the upper jaw (e). Use a drawknife to round up and trim everything.

Now cut two horns of the shape in Fig. 90. They are all the better if of curved wood. Drive their dowels into the holes prepared (a and b); and secure the horns by driving a couple of finishing nails through the skull into the dowels. If there is a visible gap between the horn-core and the skull, fill it up by wrapping soft twine into it around the core or dowel.

Give the whole thing a coat of white paint, and the skull is ready.

I have always found these skulls wonderfully decorative around the camp. Still another use was discovered. I hollowed out a space 4 × 4 inches in the back of the skull, and about 2 inches deep; then prolonged the eye-hole into this, covering the little chamber at the back with a board, somewhat hollowed in the middle, and so arranged as to make the chamber 3 inches wide. In other words, I turned the skull into a bird-box. Next year, we found every one of these hollow skulls with a pair of nesting birds—most of them wrens, but one a great-crested flycatcher.

The buffalo skull was not only a sacred symbol in the old Plains Indian camps, it was a universal and beautiful decoration. As such we use it, and never fail to find it carrying with it some of the best Indian spirit.

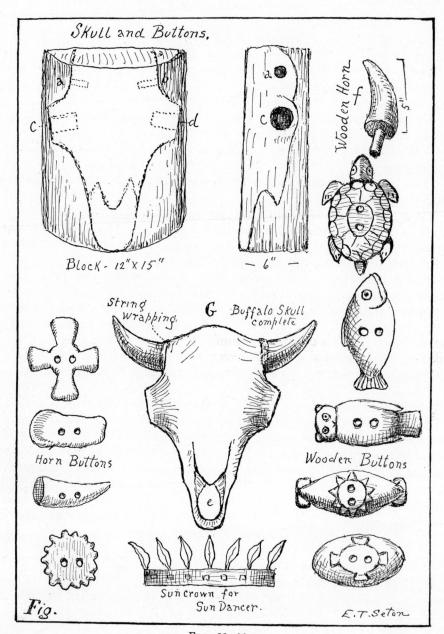

Skull and Buttons.

a   b

c   d

Block - 12" x 15"

— 6" —

a

c

Wooden Horn

f

5"

string
wrapping

G   Buffalo Skull
complete

Horn Buttons

Wooden Buttons

e

Sun crown for
Sun Dancer.

Fig.

E. T. Seton

FIGS. 89, 90.

Drums and Shields

In the *Book of Woodcraft*, I have given instructions for the making of both drums and shields, but have not gone into full details of the decoration.

The accompanying Plate (Fig. 91) offers eight designs which are Indian; that is, of Indian elements, although no one of them is an exact copy of an Indian design, so that each is authentic in detail, but not in its entirety.

I found that the most beautiful Indian designs were too complex for general use; and no one wants those that are not beautiful.

These are offered as equally suitable for drum head or shield.

As in the other Plates, horizontal lining means blue; upright, red; black is given as black or double cross-hatched lines; spotting is yellow; short upright lines mean the ground color of yellow or brownish, as wood or leather.

An experienced artist should feel free to make such changes in color as appeal to his taste; but not in the forms.

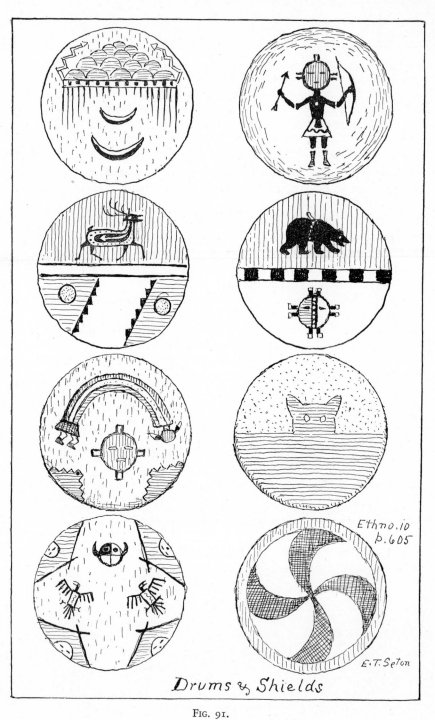

Drums & Shields

Ethno.10
p.605

E.T.Seton

FIG. 91.

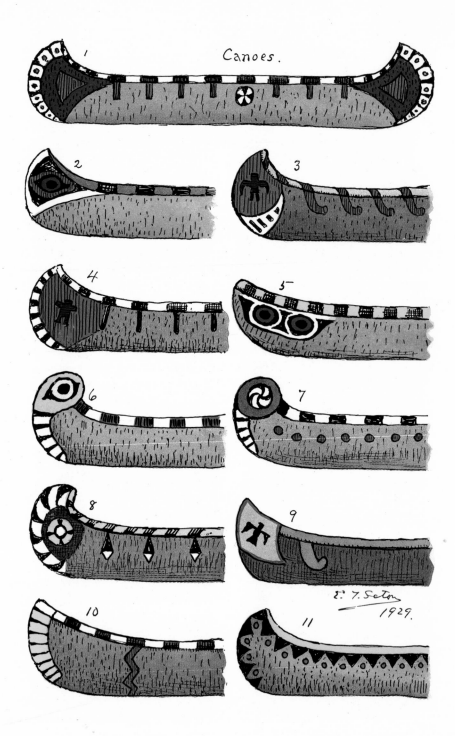

Canoes.

E. T. Seton
1929.

Canoe Decoration

Of all the craft that sail on inland waters, the canoe is the queen. For beauty of line and color, for grace, for pleasantness, and for poetry, the birch canoe, the Redman's boat, is easily the wearer of the laurel crown.

Of all the gifts that the Redman brought the world, the canoe alone was quite unique in this; it was quite perfect at the beginning; and so new in our world of thought that we had no name for it, but accepted the name its wood-haunting maker bestowed on it—*canot, kahnu,* etc.

Its every part came from the forest—birch bark cover, cedar ribs, spruce root binding, and spruce gum caulking, maple or spruce paddles.

It was perfected before the White man came—and he has not helped it since, though he has used it in every part of its native range, preferring it to any other little craft that tried to take its place.

But another enemy appeared—not a rival, but a deadly foe—the settler's axe. There was a time when millions of huge canoe birches stood in the forest—big, smooth, unblemished, ideal for the outer skin. But that day is gone; it is hard to find a birch today whose rind is good enough to make a canoe.

The cedar ribs, the spruce roots (*wattap*), the resin gum are still to be found, but the big, smooth birches are few and far between. And the White man has had to make his annual output of canoes of canvas and paint on the old cedar frame. The imitation is not bad; it is strong and waterproof, but very heavy, and difficult to repair in the wilderness.

The Indian loved and decorated everything in his life; and his embellishment of the canoe was the truest kind of art because it followed what was suggested by the structural lines and fabric of the canoe itself.

Most of the canoes in Fig. 92 have the dark and light beading on the gunwale; this is imposed by the spruce root wrapping. The triangular inset at bow and stern are the inevitable bindings of the parts; and the black upright bands on each side are the gum lines of the joints. The star of colored roots on the prow is a gratuitous embellishment or an owner's mark; and, of course, the background for it all is the exquisite varied leaf-brown of the bark itself.

And what did the White man do with this opportunity before him? With his natural genius for uglification he carried his own canoe as far as possible from the original. The lines he was bound to follow; but for the exquisite tints, colors, and patterns of the Redman, he substituted a hideous, monotonous, unvaried drab, chrome green, or sooty gray.

In the hope of adding some color joy to the outside of our funereal canoes I offer the following designs—none of them a full and exact copy of an Indian canoe, but all of the decorative elements taken from Indian sources.

The speckling of short upright scratches means ground color, usually a tan or golden brown. The black and white are indicated; and upright lining means red, as on the other Plates. Both sides and both ends of the canoe are here supposed to be alike.

Painted Paddles

All the painted paddles I ever saw came from the West Coast. So far as I know, only the West Coast Indians and their kin, the Eskimos of Alaska, ever decorated their paddles.

This was quite reasonable in them, for the paddle was as much an essential part of their lives as the bow or spear. But the Ojibway and Iroquois were paddle Indians; and, yet, up to date, I have seen no paddle of their make that was elaborately decorated.

In Fig. 93 the paddles of the upper row are of authentic Indian and Eskimo design as indicated—the Eskimo from Nelson's *Eskimos of Bering Strait*; the Indian from specimens in my own collection.

The decorations are doubtless symbolic or talismanic; but no explanation is at hand.

The lower row presents adaptations made by myself. In actual practice the Indian designs are too elaborate or complex for our life of hurry, so I found it best to simplify them, maintaining as far as possible the symbols and traditions.

Each paddle is assumed to be, first of all, of yellow varnished wood. This gives a good as well as a usual background. The designs are mostly in red and black, with occasional green; and in most cases, the color is outlined in black or in white. Red is indicated by upright lines, as in the Moccasin Plate; black by solid black or by cross-hatching; green is diagonal lines from the top down to right. In many cases, the inner ring of the eye is put in with solid white. Usually the two sides of the paddle are nearly alike.

In each case, the color enclosed by an outline should be different from the adjoining background. This is a principle of art that the Indian recognized instinctively.

The colors of the lower six may be varied at the choice of the painter, but beware of any attempt at realism.

The broad-nosed paddles are usually for deep water; the narrow and sharpened paddles are frequently used as pushers in shallow places.

It would be fine if some canoe camp would win the name of the Tribe of the Painted Paddles, by being the first to have every paddle in camp decorated with a typical Indian design.

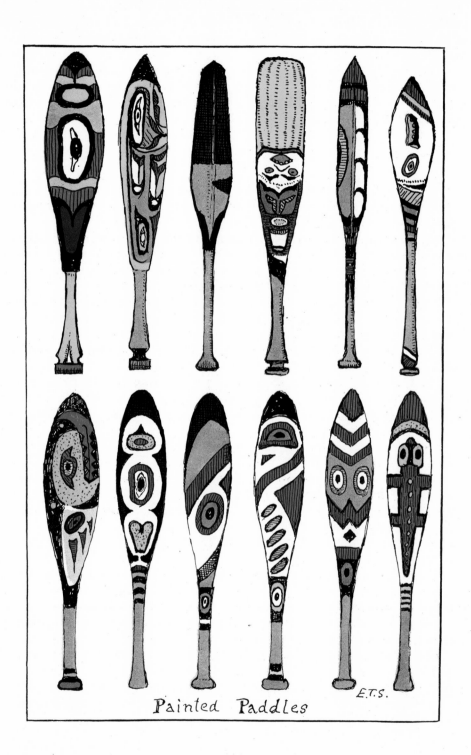

Painted Paddles

E.T.S.

The Peace Pipe

So far as I know, the American Indian is the only race that makes a solemn ceremony of smoking the pipe. The origin of this custom is surmisable, if not provable.

Incense has always been the symbol of prayer; it rises from the mystery of the Fire below, and ascends to be lost in the mystery of the All Above, the Home of the Great Mystery.

The first easily handled smokes were in the form of a fire-bowl or censer. These burned better when a hole was made near the bottom through which the priest could blow, so as to nurse the fire.

By chance, probably, he found that he could stimulate it better by drawing, especially if it were lighted with a live coal laid on top. This practice became pleasant in time, especially since it further glorified the priest by having the holy smoke proceed from his own mouth and nostrils.

This explanation is only my theory, but is supported by so many facts and probabilities that I consider it sound.

It should be a pleasant thought for our smokers, our imitators of the Redman, that in smoking they are not merely indulging in a doubtful habit, they are burning incense to the Great Mystery—they are giving upmounting wings to their secret prayer.

* * *

The ceremony of smoking the Peace Pipe—and remember it was always a peace pipe, never a war pipe—differed greatly among the various tribes. By selecting elements from the tribes I best knew, I have assembled the Chief's part in the Peace Pipe Ceremony as it appears on p. 165. This is suitable for use in the councils of the Woodcraft Indians.

The Making of the Peace Pipe

The ideal peace pipe has a bowl of the red pipestone (claystone or catlinite) that is found in the famous Pipestone Quarry of southwestern Minnesota. This deposit, when first quarried, is so soft as to be readily carved with a knife; and later turns hard with exposure.

But I have seen primitive pipe bowls made of soapstone, terra cotta, bone and wood. Since the White man came, many have been made of metal. These were commonly a combination of tomahawk for war on one side, and pipe for peace on the other; so that the mere act of smoking the peace pipe entailed burying the hatchet, the opposite edge.

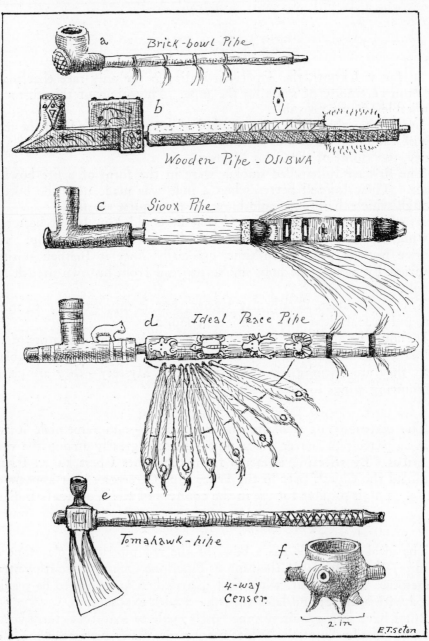

a   Brick-bowl Pipe

b   Wooden Pipe - OSIBWA

c   Sioux Pipe

d   Ideal Peace Pipe

e   Tomahawk-pipe

f   4-way Censer.

2 in.

E.T.Seton

FIG. 94.

When, in 1874, as a fourteen-year-old boy, I founded my first group of Woodcrafters, I made the official peace pipe myself. The bowl I carved out of a soft red brick; the stem I made of a long piece of elder, from which the pith was easily punched. A portrait of this pipe is given in Fig. 94 (a).

Since those days, I have made one or two peace pipes, and gathered a collection of authentic Indian examples.

Many of our campers want to make a sacred pipe for themselves. At once, they are up against the problem of boring the stem. There are five different answers to this:

(1) Use a hollow reed or bamboo of the required length; that is, about 20 inches. This undoubtedly was the original method; for the stems, and by inclusion, the whole pipe, is still called the *calumet*, which is old French for a hollow reed (Latin *calamus*).

(2) Use a hollow bone, such as the leg bone of a deer, or the wing bone of a large bird.

(3) Cut a stem out of maple, willow, poplar, or other splittable wood. Split it down the middle, dig out a central channel in one piece, then glue and lash the two pieces together again. The joint is easily hidden.

(4) Having selected the stem piece, flatten the upper surface for the whole length. In this, cut a deep, narrow groove, say ¼ inch wide and deep. Finally, cover this with a thin strip of wood, reaching the whole length, and glued as well as lashed on. The lashings may be of ornamental stuff, such as beadstrings, porky quills, or colored threads.

(5) This is by far the most used in modern times. Select for stem some sapling with a well-developed pith. In various parts of the country, different species will suggest themselves. Personally, I have used white ash, sumach (either staghorn or smooth), and elder. Cut a piece 24 inches long and 1½ to 2 inches thick, as straight and free from knots as may be. Peel the bark, trim it down a little to make sure that it has no bad flaw. Then, with a wire heated red-hot at the tip, burn out the pith, working from both ends; so that a wire 14 inches long will burn the hole through a 24-inch stem. The best size of wire is 3/16 inch thick. If heavier, it makes too large a hole; if smaller, it carries so little heat that the operation is slow.

Among the Indians, the cleaning-rod of a rifle was the wire most used. Of the twelve peace pipes now lying on my desk as I write, every one has a stem bored in this way.

I have known hours spent in boring a green ash stem; but also, I have several times bored sumach or elder stems in a minute each. Elder is by far the easiest to handle, especially when dry; but the difficulty is to get a piece of elder thick enough.

The decoration of the stem offers endless scope for individual taste; but I should advise the beginner to stick closely to some authentic pattern.

The Peace Pipe officially used when I was admitted to the Sioux nation at Standing Rock is shown in Fig. 94 at (c). The stem is of ash, and is 18 inches long. In the Plate I have indicated the decoration— bands of colored porky quills at each end; the skin and feathers from a mallard's neck, yellow ribbons, and a red-dyed horsehair tuft in the middle. The duck neck feathers are an important traditional decoration; the porky quills are red, white, blue, and yellow, gorgeous as aniline dyes can make them.

The stem is shown separate from the pipe and edge up because, when joined to the bowl, it is flat side up.

In Fig. 94, (a) is the peace pipe which I made as a boy. Its head was carved out of a soft red brick; the stem is of elder.

(b) is a pipe which I bought from an Indian in Winnipeg in January, 1887. The bowl is made of wood, lined with tin. It is painted black and decorated with lines that are incised and filled with red or yellow paint. The bosses are brass-headed tacks. The stem is of ash; and is shown in section just above. When first I got it, it had a piece of otter skin wrapped around near the mouth end.

(c) is the Sioux pipe already described.

(d) is a model peace pipe, composed of elements from many different examples—all of them authentic, and all of Plains Indian origin. The bowl is of red pipestone, inlaid with bands of soft metal supposed to be galena. The stem is separated and turned on edge to show the relief carving on the upper side. In the original, these carvings were twice as far apart. The corona of feathers hangs straight down. The feathers are strung together on two strong threads which are fastened to the under side of the stem. The feathers are white, with a spot of red sealing wax holding streamers of yellow hair on to the tip of each.

(e) is one of the war and peace tomahawk-pipes, copied from Catlin. So far as I can learn, the construction of pipe and hatchet in the same weapon was unknown before the coming of the White man.

(f) In the lower right-hand corner of the Plate is a four-way censer, of ancient type. This has four draught-holes to the fire. It typifies the fourfold fire of the Woodcraft Indians, as well as illustrates the oldest known type of fire-pot. It was given to me by J. E. Steere, of Charlotte, N. C. It is made of burnt clay, and was a usual type among the Indians of that region.

When I was quite a youngster, I wrote the following:

They Were Nigh Kin

An Injun got his dander up,
    And vowed he'd do some killin';
He tied a stone upon a stick,
    To do it with (the villain)!

He made it tight with thongs, and bright
　With paint and beads galore;
He bound a thong to hang it on—
　And lo! his club of war.

But as he worked with all his might,
　His dander simmered down;
He'd spent his fury on the club,
　He couldn't even frown.

And so he trimmed it down a bit,
　Drilled holes for fire and smoke;
He grinned, and added feather fringe,
　And even made a joke.

He added other symbols now,
　Gave merriment new lease;
He filled the bowl with spark and coal—
　And lo! the pipe of peace.

The Spirit of Woodcraft.

Bibliography

Alexander, Hartley B., Manitou Masks, E. P. Dutton & Co., 1925.

Applegate, Frank G., Indian Stories from the Pueblos, J. B. Lippincott Co., 1929.

Austin, Mary, The American Rhythm, Harcourt, Brace & Co., 1923.

Barrett, Samuel A., Ceremonies of the Pomo Indians, Univ. of Calif. Press, *Amer. Arch. & Eth.,* Vol. XII, No. 10, 1917.

Bourke, John G., Medicine Men of the Apache, 9th Ann. Rep. Bur. Eth., pp. 451-495, 1892.

Buffalo Child Long Lance, Long Lance, Cosmopolitan Book Corp., 1928.

Burton, Frederick R., American Primitive Music, Moffat, Yard & Co., 1909.

Cassidy, Ina Sizer, How Fire was Brought to the Navaho Indians, Sesame Pub. Co., Vienna-Leipzig, 1927.

Coolidge, Mary Roberts, The Rain Makers, Houghton, Mifflin Co., 1929.

Crane, Leo, Desert Drums, Little, Brown & Co., 1928.

Curtis, Natalie, The Indians' Book, Harper & Bros., 1907.

De Huff, Elizabeth, and Grunn, Homer, From Desert & Pueblo, 1924.

Densmore, Frances, American Indians and Their Music, Woman's Press, 1926.

———, Chippewa Music, Bull. 45, Bur. Eth., 1910.

———, Chippewa Music II, Bull. 53, Bur. Eth., 1913.

———, Geronimo's Song, *Indian School Journal,* April, 1906.

———, Indian Action Songs, 1922.

———, Indian Music, *Native American,* March 26, 1921.

———, Mandan and Hidatsa Music, Bull. 80, Bur. Eth., 1923.

———, Music in Its Relation to the Religious Thought of the Teton Sioux, Holmes Anniversary Volume, 1916.

———, Northern Ute Music, Bull. 75, Bur. Eth., 1922.

———, Papago Music, Bull 90, Bur. Eth., 1929.

———, Scale Formation in Primitive Music, *American Anthropologist,* Jan.-March, 1909.

———, Teton Sioux Music, Bull. 61, Bur. Eth., 1918.

Dorsey, George A., The Cheyenne, the Sun Dance, II, Field Columbia Museum, Pub. 103, Vol. IX, No. 2, 1905.

Eastman, Charles A., Soul of the Indian, Houghton, Mifflin Co., 1911.

Farwell, Arthur, National Movement for American Music, *Review of Reviews,* Dec., 1908.

Fillmore, John Comfort, Study of Indian Music, *Century Magazine,* Feb., 1894.

Fletcher, Alice C., The Hako: A Pawnee Ceremony, 22nd Ann. Rep. Bur. Eth., Part II, pp. 13-372, 1904.

———, Indian Games and Dances with Native Songs, C. C. Birchard & Co., 1915.

———, Indian Songs, *Century Magazine,* Jan., 1894.

———, Indian Story and Song from North America, Small, Maynard & Co., 1900.

———, The Omaha Tribe, 27th Ann. Rep. Bur. Eth., pp. 15-672, 1911 (with Francis La Flesche).

Grunn, Homer, see De Huff, Elizabeth.

Hambly, Wilfred D., Tribal Dancing and Social Development, Witherby, London, 1926.

Hartley, Marsden, Scientific Aesthetic of the Redman, *Art & Archaeology,* pp. 113-119, March, 1922.

Henderson, Alice Corbin, Dance Rituals of the Pueblo Indians, *Theatre Arts Monthly,* April, 1923.

Hewett, Edgar L., Native American Artists, *Art & Archaeology,* pp. 103-112, March, 1922.

Hodge, Frederick W., Handbook of the American Indians, Bull. 30, Bur. Eth., Part I, 1907; Part II, 1910.

Hoffman, Walter James, Menominee Indians, 14th Ann. Rep. Bur. Eth., Part I, pp. 11-328, 1896.

Humphrey, Rev. William Brewster, Native Melodies, Young People's Missionary Movement, 1911.

———, North American Indian Folklore Music, American Indian League, 1911.

La Flesche, Francis, Osage Tribe; Rite of Vigil, 39th Ann. Rep. Bur. Eth., 1925; also see Fletcher, Alice C.

Lawrence, D. H., Dance of the Sprouting Corn, *Theatre Arts Monthly,* July, 1924.
————, Hopi Snake Dance, *Theatre Arts Monthly,* Dec., 1924.
Literary Digest Editorial, Taking the Indianism Out of the Indian, Apr. 28, 1923.
Lummis, Charles F., Land of Poco Tiempo, Charles Scribner's Sons, 1893.
Marsh, Agnes L. and Lucile, Dance in Education, A. S. Barnes & Co., 1924.
Matthews, Dr. Washington, The Mountain Chant, a Navaho Ceremony, 5th Ann. Rep. Bur. Eth.,
    pp. 379-467, 1887.
Mooney, James, The Ghost Dance Religion, 14th Ann. Rep. Bur. Eth., Part II, pp. 641-1136, 1896.
Murdoch, John, Ethnological Results of the Point Barrow Expedition, 9th Ann. Rep. Bur. Eth., pp.
    19-441, 1892.
Nelson, Edward W., Eskimo about Bering Strait, 18th Ann. Rep. Bur. Eth., Part I, pp. 19-518, 1899.
Riggs, Stephen Return, Dakota Grammar, Texts, and Ethnology, Contributions to North American
    Ethnology, Vol. IX, 1893.
Roberts, Helen, Indian Music from the Southwest, *Natural History Mag.,* pp. 257-265, May-June,
    1927.
Salomon, Julian H., Book of Indian Crafts and Indian Lore, Harper & Bros., 1928.
Saunders, Charles F., Indians of the Terraced Houses, Putnam's Sons, 1912.
School of American Research, Fiesta Book, 1926.
Sedgwick, Mrs. William T., Acoma, the Sky City, Harvard Univ. Press, 1926.
Serviss, Garrett P., Astronomy with an Opera Glass, Appleton, 1912.
Seton, Ernest Thompson, Birch Bark Rolls of Woodcraft, 1902-1927.
Shawn, Ted, The American Ballet, Henry Holt & Co., 1926.

Chronological Bibliography

1887—The Mountain Chant, a Navaho Ceremony, by Dr. Washington Matthews, 5th Annual Report Bureau Ethnology, pp. 379–467.

1892—The Medicine Men of the Apache, by John G. Bourke, 9th Annual Report Bureau of Ethnology, pp. 451–495.

1892—Ethnological Results of the Point Barrow Expedition, by John Murdoch, 9th Annual Report Bureau Ethnology, pp. 19–441.

1893—Dakota Grammar, Texts, and Ethnology, by Stephen Return Riggs, Contributions to North American Ethnology, Vol. IX.

1893—Land of Poco Tiempo, by Charles F. Lummis, Charles Scribner's Sons.

1894—Indian Songs, by Alice C. Fletcher, *Century Magazine*, Jan.

1894—A Study of Indian Music, by John Comfort Fillmore, *Century Magazine*, Feb.

1896—The Menominee Indians, by Walter James Hoffman, 14 Annual Report Bureau Ethnology, Part I, pp. 11–328.

1896—The Ghost Dance Religion, by James Mooney, 14th Annual Report Bureau Ethnology, Part II, pp. 641–1136.

1899—The Eskimo About Bering Strait, by Edward W. Nelson, 18th Annual Report Bureau Ethnology, Part I, pp. 19–518.

1900—Indian Story and Song from North America, by Alice C. Fletcher, Small, Maynard & Co.

1902–1927—The Birch Bark Rolls of Woodcraft, by Ernest Thompson Seton.

1904—The Hako: A Pawnee Ceremony, by Alice C. Fletcher, 22nd Annual Report Bureau Ethnology, Part II, pp. 13–372.

1905—The Cheyenne, The Sun Dance, II, by George A. Dorsey, Field Columbian Museum, Publication 103, Vol. IX, No. 2.

1906—Geronimo's Song, by Frances Densmore, *Indian School Journal*, April.

1907—Handbook of the American Indians, Bull. 30, Part I, Bureau of American Ethnology, edited by Frederick W. Hodge.

1907—The Indians' Book, by Natalie Curtis, Harper & Bros.

1908—A National Movement for American Music, by Arthur Farwell, *Review of Reviews*, Dec.

1909—Scale Formation in Primitive Music, by Frances Densmore, *American Anthropologist*, Jan.-March.

1909—American Primitive Music, by Frederick R. Burton, Moffat, Yard & Co.

1910—Handbook of the American Indians, Bull. 30, Part II, Bureau of American Ethnology, edited by Frederick W. Hodge.

1910—Chippewa Music, by Frances Densmore, Bull. 45, Bureau Ethnology.

1911—North American Indian Folklore Music, prepared by Rev. William Brewster Humphrey, pub. by American Indian League, N. Y.

1911—The Omaha Tribe, by Alice C. Fletcher, and Francis La Flesche, 27th Annual Report Bureau Ethnology, pp. 15–672.

1911—Native Melodies, collected by Rev. William Brewster Humphrey, pub. by Young People's Missionary Movement, N. Y.

1911—Soul of the Indian, by Charles A. Eastman (Ohiyesa), Houghton, Mifflin Co.

1912—Astronomy with an Opera Glass, by Garrett P. Serviss. Appleton.

1912—Indians of the Terraced Houses, by Charles F. Saunders, G. P. Putnam's Sons.

1913—Chippewa Music, II, by Frances Densmore, Bull. 53, Bureau Ethnology.

1915—Indian Games and Dances, with Native Songs, by Alice C. Fletcher, C. C. Birchard & Co.

1916—Music in its Relation to the Religious Thought of the Teton Sioux, by Frances Densmore, Holmes Anniversary Volume, Wash.

1917—Ceremonies of the Pomo Indians, by Samuel A. Barrett, Univ. of Calif. Press, Amer. Arch. & Eth., Vol. XII, No. 10.

1918—Teton Sioux Music, by Frances Densmore, Bull. 61, Bureau Ethnology.

1921—Indian Music, by Frances Densmore, *Native American*, March 26th.

1922—The Scientific Aesthetic of the Redman, by Marsden Hartley, *Art & Archaeology*, March, pp. 113–119.

1922—Native American Artists, by Dr. Edgar L. Hewett, *Art & Archaeology*, March, pp. 103–112.

1922—Indian Action Songs, by Frances Densmore.

1922—Northern Ute Music, by Frances Densmore, Bull. 75, Bureau Ethnology.

1923—Mandan and Hidatsa Music, by Frances Densmore, Bull. 80, Bureau Ethnology.

1923—Taking the Indianism out of the Indian, *Literary Digest*, April 28th.

1923—The Dance Rituals of the Pueblo Indians, by Alice C. Henderson, *Theatre Arts Monthly*, April.

1923—The American Rhythm, by Mary Austin, Harcourt, Brace & Co.

1924—From Desert and Pueblo, collected and transcribed by Elizabeth W. De Huff and Homer Grunn.

1924—The Dance of the Sprouting Corn, by D. H. Lawrence, *Theatre Arts Monthly*, July.

1924—The Hopi Snake Dance, by D. H. Lawrence, *Theatre Arts Monthly*, Dec.

1925—Manitou Masks, by Hartley B. Alexander, E. P. Dutton & Co.

1925—The Osage Tribe; Rite of Vigil, by Francis La Flesche, 39th Annual Report Bureau Ethnology, pp. 31–636.

1926—Tribal Dancing and Social Development, by Wilfred D. Hambly, Witherby.

1926—The American Ballet, by Ted Shawn, Henry Holt & Co.

1926—The American Indians and their Music, by Frances Densmore, Woman's Press.

1926—The Fiesta Book, Papers of the School of American Research, pp. 44–57.

1926—Acoma, the Sky City, by Mrs. William T. Sedgwick, Harvard Univ. Press.

1927—How Fire was Brought to the Navaho Indians, by Ina Sizer Cassidy, Sesame Pub. Co., Vienna-Leipzig.

1927—Indian Music from the Southwest, by Helen Roberts, *Natural History Mag.*, May-June, pp. 257–265.

1928—Long Lance, by Chief Buffalo Child Long Lance, Cosmopolitan Book Corp.

1928—Book of Indian Crafts and Indian Lore, by Julian H. Salomon, Harper & Bros.

1928—Desert Drums, by Leo Crane, Little, Brown & Co.

1929—Indian Stories from the Pueblos, by Frank G. Applegate, J. B. Lippincott Co.

1929—The Rain Makers, by Mary Roberts Coolidge, Houghton, Mifflin Co.

1929—Papago Music, by Frances Densmore, Bull. 90, Bureau Ethnology.

Songs According to Tribes

268

Alphabetical List of Songs

INDEX